THE ART OF WRITING A NON-FICTION BOOK

AN EASY GUIDE TO RESEARCHING, CREATING, EDITING, AND SELF-PUBLISHING YOUR FIRST BOOK

BRYAN COLLINS

BECOME A *Writer* TODAY

PREFACE

This book uses British English.
Thank you for supporting this work.

CONTENTS

Preface iii
Get Your Exclusive Bonus vii
Page One ix
The 7 Most Common Mistakes of Aspiring Non-Fiction Authors .. xiii

Part I
BECOMING A NON-FICTION AUTHOR

1. So You Want to Write Your First Book? 3
2. Finding Out What Your Readers Expect (and Who They Are) .. 12
3. Learning to Express Yourself Faster 21
4. Taking Charge of Your Tools Before They Take Charge of You .. 29
5. Knowing When It's Time to Write (and Finding Space to Do It) .. 39

Part II
WRITING YOUR NON-FICTION BOOK

6. Finding More Ideas Than You Know What to Do With 49
7. Researching Your Book: The Nobel Prize Approach 57
8. Cracking the Book Outlining Code 67
9. Taming That Unruly First Draft 78
10. Mastering Your Writing Self Like a Zen Master 87
11. Self-Editing Your Book Until It's Good Enough to Publish .. 95

Part III
FINDING LASTING SUCCESS WITH YOUR BOOK

12. Acting on Critical Feedback (without Losing Your Mind) .. 107
13. Picking a Best-Selling Title for Your Book 115
14. Self-Publishing Your Non-Fiction Book Like a Pro 124
15. Finishing (and Shipping) Your Book 134

16. Free, Free at Last! 142
    The END 150

Top Tools and Resources for Today's Authors 153
Remember Your Bonus 161
Become a Writer Today 163
The Power of Creativity 165
About the Author 167
Acknowledgments 171
References 173

GET YOUR EXCLUSIVE BONUS

I've created a **FREE video masterclass** that you should check out now before you start reading. It will help cut months off how long it takes you to write your book, using my best tactics and strategies.

WAIT!
DID YOU CLAIM YOUR FREE BONUS?

VISIT
BECOMEAWRITERTODAY.COM/AUTHOR

If you want to get this masterclass, visit http://becomeawritertoday.com/author

PAGE ONE

It's in your hands.

You lift the pages up to your nose and can almost smell the ink. This is a victory. It's the culmination of months of editing, writing, research, revisions and sacrifices.

You've done something most aspiring creative people put off. You've stopped talking about having a book inside you that you'll write *one day*, got the words out of your head and onto the blank page. You've shaped, edited and revised your book and then had the guts to release it into the world.

Flicking through page after page, you're amazed you possessed the mental discipline to write it and proud you saw the idea through. You should be too.

But what if you're not there yet?

What if you've spent months or even years writing your non-fiction book, but it's still languishing inside your computer or drawer.

It's unfinished, unpublished and a painful reminder of how far you still must go.

When you sit down to write, you wonder: *Is this a waste of time? Why can't I write my book? Am I ever going to become an author?*

It's enough to make you want to give up writing altogether.

I'll let you in on a secret: you're not alone.

Like you, I'd been dreaming about writing a book for years. But every day, I woke up and something got in the way: kids, a job, the front doorbell ringing and more.

My friends would ask me, "Is your book finished yet?" And I'd reply, "It's coming along."

I spent years talking about writing this mythical book, but I didn't know how to finish it. I felt tired and embarrassed by my lack of progress.

I knew I could have written the book inside of me had I taken a different approach. So I studied what successful non-fiction authors do, and I changed how I wrote. Now, I want to share what I learnt about writing a non-fiction book with you.

WHAT THIS BOOK WILL TEACH YOU

This book offers practical, real-world advice for new writers and aspiring non-fiction authors. It's suitable for you if you have an idea you want to turn into a book and if you've never written a book before.

In the **first part of this book**, you'll discover what it takes to become a non-fiction author. I tackle how to find ideas if you don't have any, how to organise them and express yourself.

Then, I'll cover how to get your messy first draft out of your head and onto the blank page. I'll also go cover the one thing you shouldn't do while researching and writing your first draft.

If writing non-fiction books is already your thing, there are still a few technical and a few craft-related skills you must acquire.

Don't let this put you off.

In the **second part** of this book, I'll explain how to gain the skills you need to write your book. You'll learn how to master research, your tools and what to do about that messy first draft.

Does writing a book sound like it will take up a lot of time?

I get it. I wrote my first two non-fiction books around the margins of the day while balancing a full-time job, two small children, a wife, friends and so on.

As an aspiring author, you may lack the time and freedom to work on your book full-time. I'll explain how to master your free hours for writing and set up your environment for success.

I'll also tackle how to cultivate the mental discipline it takes to write a book by mastering the one thing you have complete control over: yourself.

Because hey, creating a book is tough. Once you finish writing your first or second draft, it's time to edit and revise your manuscript.

Many new writers have trouble with editing and revisions. Their editor sends them back the manuscript covered in annotations, and the writer wonders...

How will I ever finish this?

How will I ever write something readers will want, let alone pay for?

I won't lie, critical feedback is hard to swallow.

In the **third part** of this book, I'll tackle the ins and outs of self-editing and the art of revising your drafts. I will also explain what to expect when working with a professional editor.

Of course, if you want to sell copies of your book – what writer doesn't want to sell their book? - you'll need to publish something your readers want. So it's best to involve them early and often, and I'll explain how.

Editorial and real-world feedback are nice, but, there's no point getting stuck in a cycle of revising, editing and reworking your non-fiction book.

Don't let the siren's call of perfectionism seduce you.

You need to have a plan for finishing, shipping or self-publishing your book. Today that's easier than ever to achieve. Once you publish your book, you're free to decide what to do next.

Should you focus on earning a living from your writing, try to make an impact with your ideas, or write something new?

With a finished book in your hands, you'll have the answers you need.

You'll be an author.

THE 7 MOST COMMON MISTAKES OF ASPIRING NON-FICTION AUTHORS

It's exciting, isn't it?

Writing your first book and then sending the final version to your editor and later having it available (and SELLING!) on stores like Amazon, iTunes and Kobo.

The months (or even years) of hard work are over, and now you can watch with pride as your book goes out into the world.

Now, you can sit back as your ideas and stories make an impact on readers and earn you a side income.

You can finally call yourself an author.

But what if you're not there yet? What if you're still struggling to finish writing your first book?

Then I think you'll agree with me that trying to write a non-fiction book is tough work.

So I'm going to be honest with you and reveal seven of the most common writing mistakes aspiring non-fiction authors must avoid.

These are the writing mistakes that tripped me up before I published my first book.

If you want to become a non-fiction author, don't let them hoodwink you.

BOOK WRITING MISTAKE #1: I SHOULD WRITE DIFFERENT THINGS AT ONCE

A blog post.

An article for a magazine.

A book.

Perhaps the great American novel.

There are so many tantalising and exciting new ideas to explore.

Often new writers work on different writing projects at once, and then they struggle to make real progress.

Writing lots of things at once is fine if you're John McPhee, Malcolm Gladwell or a professional author who has been at this for years.

If you're just starting out, it's a common writing mistake.

Here's why:

According to a 2012 article in *Psychology Today*, people who jump from one task to the next are up to 40% less productive. What's more, when you multi-task or switch tasks, you incur a cognitive penalty. You perform worse than the person who brings a single-minded focus to his or her work.

Writers are no exception.

It gets worse too.

When you are working on lots of projects, you'll find it harder to create a writing routine that sticks.

What's more, you'll delay finishing your drafts and postpone the feeling of accomplishment that comes when you finally press publish.

This state is an essential reward if you're serious about your writing.

So one book at a time, please.

BOOK WRITING MISTAKE #2: I DON'T NEED TO ORGANISE IDEAS FOR MY BOOK

Did you ever think of an idea for your book and feel excited about using it?

You can't wait to put this idea into practice and start writing. But you wonder...

What if I did a little bit more research?

So you pick up the phone, open a book or a web browser, and you look into your first idea. And the next one. And the one after that.

You spend hours clicking and browsing from one blog post to the next or reading books you love. There are too many ideas to choose from.

When you have time, you scribble your notes on Post-Its, on the back of notepads and in the margins of various books. More often than not, you don't write anything down, thinking you'll remember these golden nuggets later on.

After all, isn't the human brain a magnificent organ?

Later, when it's time to write, it's a struggle to produce even 300 words because you don't know how to make sense of your research. It's in too many different places, and that great hook for a chapter you thought about in the gym... it's gone.

Successful non-fiction writers don't risk losing their best ideas. Like a doctor, lawyer or academic, they treat research seriously. They keep their ideas in one place, and they review what they find.

To write your book, you need a system (digital or otherwise) for capturing, sorting and evaluating your ideas. You shouldn't have to spend time trying to think of a scientific study you read months ago.

Instead it should sit next to anecdotes, interviews, quotes, reader surveys...and the rest of your research.

When you do this, you'll be able to write your non-fiction book, all the while knowing your best ideas are there, when you need them.

BOOK WRITING MISTAKE #3: I SHOULD WRITE MY BOOK WHEN I FEEL PASSIONATE OR INSPIRED

I'm all for feeling passionate about your creative work, but let's be logical about this...

Imagine you're training to run a marathon.

(I picked a marathon because writing a book can feel like a long, intensive slog.)

So if you want to run 26.2 miles for the first time, you can't turn up on the day of the marathon and expect to finish the race.

You've got to train when you don't want to, practice when you're tired and squeeze your sessions into your otherwise busy week.

Now, you might feel passionate about training when it's sunny outside, but what about on a cold, wet Tuesday evening?

You're going to have to do the work anyway.

The same applies to writing.

When you turn up in front of a blank page, it takes a precious amount of creative time to warm up and figure out what you're trying to say. And if you haven't practiced writing in days or weeks, it'll take even longer.

Look, inspiration and passion are nice.

There's nothing better than sitting down in front of the blank page with a hot idea and an urge to write your book.

But if you wait around all day to come up with an idea and for inspiration to strike, what will you do if nothing comes?

Will you wait until tomorrow, next week or next month for inspiration to tap you on the shoulder and say, "Hey, it's time to write chapter five of your book"?

Because that's a sure-fire way never to finish writing your book.

Believe me, I've been there.

BOOK WRITING MISTAKE #4: I SHOULD WRITE MY NON-FICTION BOOK ON THE WEEKENDS

Between your job, family and personal life, finding time to write your book is difficult.

Now, I don't want to upset you, but...

....deciding it's okay to write a chapter in your book only on the weekends is a sure-fire way to finish nothing at all.

Sure, there'll be an occasional productive Saturday morning. You'll write for two or even three hours and produce 1,000 great words.

You'll say, "That was a morning well-spent."

But what happens if you don't find time to write on a Saturday or Sunday and you miss a weekend?

Or what happens if the weekend's writing session is a flop?

It'll be an entire week before you put your butt in the chair, your hands on the keyboard and turn up in front of the blank page. And if you miss a weekend?

You're putting seven, fourteen or even twenty-one days between writing sessions.

You'll never get into the rhythm and momentum of writing your book.

I don't know about you, but I can't wait that long to finish what I started, which is why I changed how and when I write.

Getting a writing schedule in place or even finding time to write is a real struggle when you're new at this.

A writing routine you stick to will help, as will one you follow before the demands of the day take over.

Now, this brings me to...

BOOK WRITING MISTAKE #5: I WILL FINISH WRITING MY NON-FICTION BOOK IF I JUST WORK HARDER

When you're working on a book for the first time, telling yourself to 'work harder' or 'don't be lazy' is TERRIBLE advice.

Here's why:

Self-talk might get your ass in the chair on day one, but when you miss a day, you'll feel bad.

And if you miss two days, you'll feel even worse.

Then, your book becomes this BIG THING you've got to do.

Like any hard and difficult task, you'll procrastinate about it, put it off and even forget about it.

Again, this is a common writing mistake.

I once stuffed a manuscript in my drawer and 'forgot' about it for three months because I felt guilty about my lack of progress.

Yes, writing a book is tough when you're starting out (remember my marathon analogy?), but don't make it harder than it needs to be.

I discovered telling myself to 'work harder' wasn't helping me write a book and would never help me publish one. Then, I found a solution that helped me get better results.

And my secret?

Well, you need a way of breaking down your book into milestones that you can reach one by one.

You need a way of tracking your progress until you reach The End. (God, I love getting to The End.)

More on that later.

BOOK WRITING MISTAKE #6: IT'S OKAY TO EDIT AND WRITE MY BOOK AT THE SAME TIME

Have you ever written a paragraph, rewrote it, written another paragraph and then went back and rewrote that too?

And on and on and on...

An hour goes by.

You realise you have written nothing. All you've done is rewrite the same part of your book.

Ouch!

I used to write like this all the time. I spent hours tinkering with my sentences, and I often went back to perfect them.

Again. And again.

This is a terrible way to write your book.

Here's why:

When you try to write and edit at the same time, you're doing TWO different activities.

The part of your brain that must write to get ideas out of your head and organise them – your internal writer – shies away from your internal editor.

The part of your brain that turns your first draft into writing that shines – your internal editor – does his or her best work with a complete first draft.

BOOK WRITING MISTAKE #7: I SHOULD ONLY PUBLISH MY BOOK WHEN IT'S PERFECT

When I was in my mid-twenties, I wanted to write literary non-fiction.

So I enrolled in an intensive creative writing class in Dublin.

Our tutor was a balding American in his early thirties from Texas.

"Jeff," I said. "I'm struggling to finish this idea I have for a story... what do I need to do to write something great?"

"Bryan, your writing is full of clichés," he said. "You write like a 1920s pulp fiction novelist."

"I can work on that," I said. "Tell me how I can get better."

"Trying to write one true great sentence is like throwing a typewriter at the moon?"

"What do you mean?"

"It's impossible."

We laughed.

He laughed harder.

And I spent my weekends editing and rewriting the same sentences until I felt they were just right.

I threw typewriters at the moon for four years, and in that time, I finished just six short stories. Sure, they had pretty sentences, but here's the painful truth:

They were lousy.

My quest for the perfect sentence consumed me. I forgot great stories succeed because of the tale and the characters within in them.

That wasn't the worst part either.

Because I'd failed to finish a lot of my stories, it was impossible for me to get candid, real-world editorial feedback about the quality of my writing.

Much later, I learned from my painful writing mistakes, and I discovered I wasn't a fiction writer after all.

Like you, my passion was – is – writing non-fiction.

HOW TO FINALLY WRITE YOUR NON-FICTION BOOK

Sometimes, I make embarrassing and common writing mistakes.

Recently, I spent two months rewriting an old book when I should have concentrated on publishing my new book, but that's okay.

I still fall, but I read as much as I can about writing and our craft. I use what I discover to fall forwards, instead of falling down.

Now, I'll reveal what I've discovered about non-fiction book writing. I'll help you avoid these mistakes and learn from the masters of our craft.

The blank page awaits.

PART I
BECOMING A NON-FICTION AUTHOR

SO YOU WANT TO WRITE YOUR FIRST BOOK?

"The more beautifully you shape your work around one clear idea, the more meanings your audiences will discover... as they take your idea and follow its implications into every aspect of their lives." – Robert McKee

You've got competition.

According to the UK Office for National Statistics, there are over 70,000 authors, writers and translators in the UK. Meanwhile, according to the US Bureau of Labor Statistics, there are over 43,380 writers and authors in the United States

These are professional writers who publish books or get paid for their work in some form. Both figures above say nothing for the many thousands more who take creative writing classes and tell their friends over a drink that they have this great idea for a book, and how they'll write it... one day.

Like many authors, I wanted to write a book ever since I was 12 years old. When I was a teenager, I was playing football in a field near my house. After the match, one of my friends produced a marijuana cigarette (a joint) and asked if I wanted a drag.

I told him, "Words get me high!"

I first tried to write a book when I was 19, but I couldn't get past page five. I didn't understand how to keep a story moving or even how to sit in a chair for more than 30 minutes and write about one thing.

That didn't stop me from boring friends to death in the pub about my ideas for short stories, novellas and non-fiction books.

It was a lot easier to talk about becoming an author than it was to actually write a book.

I always liked the idea of writers up against the blank page and waiting for their muse or divine inspiration to strike, but those moments never came. So I spent most of my twenties figuring out successful non-fiction authors do a lot of work upfront *before they* start writing a book.

It's not enough to want to write a book. If you wish to join the ranks of professional, successful authors, start by considering why you want to write a book. Then determine what your non-fiction book is about.

WHY ARE YOU WRITING A BOOK?

Many authors don't talk about the loneliness of their craft. You spend hours researching your book, writing and rewriting it, and sit in a room with only your words and ideas for company.

In the middle of every creative project, there's a moment when your initial enthusiasm drains away. You wonder if you should continue writing your book.

Hey, it's easier to sit down in front of the television with a bowl of Häagen-Dazs and watch old shows on Netflix.

If you've never written a book, these moments of self-doubt can feel overwhelming. But they'll pass if you press forwards, one sentence at a time.

You'll face other challenges too. If the people close to you aren't writers, they won't understand what you're doing. For instance, while

I was writing this chapter, a new writer struggling to finish his book emailed me to say:

> One of the reasons I have not gone farther with writing is because my family sees me working at a computer, or like today with a cell phone, and thinks I'm goofing off.

Even the most supportive wife/husband/friend/cat/dog isn't going to be able to carry your book over the finish line. Still, there's a reason lots of authors dedicate their books to family members and friends. It takes a single-minded focus, and even a dash of selfishness, to finish writing a book.

You'll be able to recommit to writing your book and explain to others what you're doing, if you figure out *your why* in advance. To do it, ask yourself:

- Am I writing this book to improve my craft?
- Is my book a passion project?
- Is a book the best medium for me to express my ideas?
- What do I want to achieve with my book: money, recognition or to make an impact?
- Will this book help me advance my dream of writing full-time?
- Will this book help me advance my career or become an expert in my field?
- Do I want to generate a side income from my book, and if so, how much?
- How will I serve existing and/or new readers with my book?

Establish at least five to ten reasons why you're writing your non-fiction book. Over the coming months, understanding your why will help you conquer self-doubt. It will also help you answer difficult questions from others and keep writing.

WHY I WROTE THE POWER OF CREATIVITY

During 2015 and early 2016, I researched and wrote a non-fiction book for writers and artists called *The Power of Creativity*. I knew the book would be tough work. So before setting out on page one, I created *my list of whys*.

On more than one occasion, I re-read my list to overcome problems like self-doubt and not feeling motivated to write.

Here's the list:

1. I want to serve my readers with more than productivity advice. (Up until this point, I wrote articles mostly about how to get things done.)
2. Writing a book about creativity will help me become a better writer.
3. This book will give me credibility about the subject of creativity.
4. I've researched the market, and there's a demand for books about creativity.
5. I want to master the art of non-fiction storytelling.
6. Writing and shipping this book will help me clarify if I should spend my time writing fiction or non-fiction. (A question I've struggled with for years.)
7. I want to increase my side income from writing and self-publishing books.

DISCOVERING YOUR BOOK'S OBLIGATORY CONVENTIONS

When I buy a ticket to see the latest superhero film, I expect to feel awed by a hero possessing strange and unusual powers. I want him or her to get into a ridiculous costume and fight a bizarre-looking nemesis before the credits roll.

If this doesn't happen, I'll feel short-changed. The hero's origin story and their confrontation with a nemesis are two of the obligatory conventions of the superhero genre.

Every good director includes them.

Writers who exclude the obligatory conventions of their genre are short-changing their readers. But you can avoid this problem by becoming a student of the market.

Spend at least an hour browsing the Amazon categories relevant to your book, and find ones with a sales ranking below 30,000. Typically, these sell at least five copies a day, meaning they earn income for their authors.

Study the good and bad book reviews so you can see what readers like and dislike and how you can do better. I'm drawn to the three-star reviews because they're mostly written by people who aren't all-out fanboys/girls or haters.

At the end of your research, you'll know whether you're writing about a topic with few writers or wading into a genre with serious competition.

Now, perhaps your genre is underserved.

Think carefully about why nobody is writing about this topic and whether you're going to be able to sell your book.

Find would-be readers and ask them if they'll open their wallets or purses to pay for what you're about to write.

If they say yes, that's good news!

There's a demand for the book you're about to write, and these other books will help you figure out what to include and exclude.

Next, read at least five popular books in your genre. During your first read-through, enjoy the book in question. Later, go through the books again, studying the front matter, chapter titles and their lengths, the index, the conclusion and so on.

Then ask yourself:

- What's the most important idea or concept in each book?
- How does each author present information to their readers?
- How can I summarise each book?

- What are the typical word counts of the chapters and books within my niche?
- What types of research, stories and exercises (if any) do my chosen authors include?
- What's the tone of voice within each book?
- What ideas do I agree/disagree with?
- What does this book and other books include?

I answer these questions and summarise the books using a mind map (I'll address how to do this later on). As you evaluate each book, consider if you can combine these ideas with your perspective.

ESTABLISHING WHAT YOUR BOOK IS ABOUT

Writing your first non-fiction book without knowing what it's about and who it's for is like trying to cut a tree trunk in half with a rusty, old saw. If you're determined enough, you'll get there in the end, but why complicate things for yourself?

There are easier ways to write a good non-fiction book that people will pay for.

Like many new non-fiction writers, you may have a topic in mind for your book. You may want to write about a sports or diet regime, tell a personal life story or offer a guide to a complex topic like teaching science to kids.

Your job will be a hell of a lot easier if you get yourself a chainsaw.

For authors, that chainsaw is the controlling idea behind a book.

The American creative writing instructor Robert McKee introduced this concept, explaining:

> The controlling idea shapes the writer's choices. It's yet another Creative Discipline to guide your aesthetic choices toward what is appropriate or inappropriate in your story, toward what is expressive of your controlling idea and may be kept versus what is irrelevant to it and must be cut.

According to McKee, the controlling idea of the *Dirty Harry* series of films is: "Justice triumphs because the protagonist is more violent than the criminals."

Although McKee concerns himself with screenwriting (and fiction to a degree), the controlling idea applies to non-fiction writing too.

I read Joan Didion's memoir *The Year of Magical Thinking* on New Year's Eve in 2015. My wife went out with friends to the pub, and we didn't have a babysitter.

So I stayed up late at home and read about how Joan Didion's husband John Gregory Dunne died unexpectedly of a heart attack at their kitchen table in 2003.

It was a depressing way to bring in the New Year, but I couldn't put Didion's non-fiction book down. She explores the impact of grief and the nature of death by telling stories about her life before and after Dunne's death.

Didion weaves in psychological and medical research. She contrasts the story of John's death against her daughter's health problems and hospitalisation. She writes:

A single person is missing for you, and the whole world is empty.

I've no idea if Didion overtly established a controlling idea. Yet, it's clear to any reader: "No one is ready for death and it can arrive at any time with devastating consequences."

You can figure out your book's controlling idea by spending an hour asking and answering some simple questions:

- Who is my book for?
- What am I trying to say?
- Who or what is the subject of my book?
- What is the point of view of my book?
- What is the core value underpinning my book?
- How is my book different to everything else that's out there?

Your answers are for you alone, so be as honest as you can. Then, distil them into a single sentence, and pin this next to where you write. You could start your book without doing this extra work. But your controlling idea will help you avoid spending hours writing about the wrong things.

Here's the controlling idea for this very book:

> With the right ideas, skills and hard work, you can become a successful non-fiction author today.

During the editing process, your controlling idea will help you assess whether each chapter achieves its purpose. It will help you prop your book on a firm foundation.

Don't worry if you don't get your controlling idea right at the start. You can update your idea *while* writing your book.

THE PAGES AHEAD

Lots of aspiring writers sit around bars, telling their friends they have a great idea for a book. Then they order another beer, coffee or glass of wine and carry on talking without any real intention to start writing.

Then there are the would-be writers who complain they *could write a book*, but they don't have the time, they're not committed to doing it, or they don't know what their book is about... yet.

You are a different kind of writer. You know what your book is about and who it's for and you've even got a controlling idea.

Now, you're about to put together a plan for writing and publishing your non-fiction book, and that's more intoxicating than anything you can order in a bar.

YOUR WRITING EXERCISES

- Clarify why you want to write your non-fiction book and what you'd like to achieve with it.
- Spend 30-60 minutes establishing the controlling idea for your non-fiction book. Rather than trying to perfect this idea and procrastinating for weeks, adjust your controlling idea while you write.

FINDING OUT WHAT YOUR READERS EXPECT (AND WHO THEY ARE)

"Everyone wants to climb the mountain, but the big difference between those at the top and those still on the bottom is simply a matter of showing up tomorrow to give it just one more shot." – Gary Halbert

The American writer Gary Halbert (1938-2007) was a master of writing to just one person - his ideal customer. Halbert built a career and earned millions of dollars for his clients working as a copywriter and direct response marketer.

He wrote about and sold the benefits of his clients' products and services, but it was never the quiet life for Halbert. He once said:

> I have been robbed, tied up, gagged blindfolded, threatened. I've made and lost millions. I have been eulogized, ostracized, and plagiarized. I've also... been both a prison guard and a prison inmate.

Halbert's father died when he was 57 years of age, and Halbert was always afraid of facing the same fate. So at the age of 46, Halbert decided to teach his son, Bond, all he knew about earning a living and getting by.

At the time, Halbert was serving a ten-month prison sentence in a federal prison camp in California. Prison isn't the most conducive environment for a father-son relationships. So Halbert used the single most powerful tool at his disposal to teach Bond what he knew – the written word.

During his stretch inside, Halbert sent Bond over 25 letters – each several hundred words long.

In the letters, Halbert tackled topics like "How to keep going when the going is hard!", "The surest way to become a big money writer!" and "How to get flowing again when you are stuck!"

The ultimate salesman, Halbert even offered his son "an emotional 'tool kit' which can save your life!"

Much later, Bond gathered his father's writings and published them as *The Boron Letters*.

When I first read this book, Halbert struck me as a copywriter focused on adding to his bottom line, but then I dug a little deeper into his letters. The letters are less about earning a living than they are about learning **how to live**.

In one letter, Halbert describes losing himself to a song on the radio. A roommate shattered his brief mental respite from prison, screamed at Halbert to turn off the radio and threatened him.

Gary, a big and physical man, wasn't the kind of inmate "to get sand kicked in his face", and he considered fighting his roommate.

He knew one or both of them would get hurt and that this would complicate things for himself and Bond in the long term. So Halbert kept silent, turned off the radio and "ate humble pie".

Halbert wrote to his son about this ugly confrontation. He told Bond to avoid emotional decisions when feeling hungry, angry, lonely or tired.

"What should you do?" he asks his son. "What I did. Write, run, walk, talk, jog etc."

In a reply, Bond thanks his father for this advice and says he now waits 72 hours before making big decisions.

"This little rule has saved me a ton of grief," says Bond.

It's saved thousands of other readers a lot of grief too, but Halbert didn't write his letters for thousands of readers: he wrote them for his son.

Today, *The Boron Letters* is a cult-classic for copywriters and marketers seeking to discover more than just how to earn a fast buck. The letters are an instruction manual for living, and they succeed because Halbert wrote for his ideal reader first.

Halbert begins almost every letter with "Dear Bond" and ends with "I love you and good luck! Dad."

He knew exactly who he was writing to, and unless you're into the cliché of the penniless artist, you should write for your ideal reader too.

DETERMINING WHO YOUR IDEAL READER IS (AND WHAT THEY WANT)

If you're writing a book about fitness, it's not enough to write for men and women aged 18-65. That's too broad and open, and your book will get pneumonia.

For example, I typically write for men and women with a college education. They are aged between 30-50, and they live in the United States, Ireland, Canada and the United Kingdom. They are primarily new writers too.

And if I'm honest, that's a little broad.

My audience is new writers, and solving their problems informs many of the chapters in this book.

Remember, narrow and deep is better than wide and shallow. Halbert went so narrow and deep that he only wrote to one person – his son.

Don't gaze out the window and wait for a divine insight. Go to where your readers hang out. And no, I'm not talking about skulking around your local library.

If you have readers, ask them what they need help with.

Check your blog or website analytics, and figure out what posts are most popular. Then use this information to determine what you should write more or less of.

Send your readers an email or a short survey. For example, I ask readers who subscribe to my email list this question: "What are you struggling with right now?"

Over the past twelve months, I have received answers like:

- "My biggest struggle as a time-strapped blogger is finding the right balance between editing to perfection and publishing as is."
- "When I'm writing, the biggest frustration is distraction."
- "I feel like I'm at the stage where I need someone to keep me accountable, someone who is a writer and understands."
- "For me, writing is easy. The ideas, dialogue, scenes are all in my head waiting to pour out through my fingers. The frustrating part is finding the time to make this happen."

If you don't have readers, you'll need to find and interview three potential readers of a book like yours. Ask yourself:

- What kind of person would read my book?
- Who do I know that represents my ideal reader?
- Who can introduce me to my ideal reader?

Reach out to people on relevant Facebook groups, to your LinkedIn connections and to your personal network.

The question and answer site Quora is also a great source of reader information. There, you can see the real-world problems of your target audience and what they respond to. While researching this book on Quora, I came across questions like:

- "Do writers ever run out of ideas about what to write about? And what do they do to overcome this?
- "What makes a writer great?"

- "As a writer, how does it feel to be suffering from writer's block?"

It's always best to ask real people about your idea before writing a non-fiction book. You can conduct these reader interviews over Skype, the phone or face-to-face.

Explain that you're writing a book about [insert topic] and that you need their help and value real-world feedback. Remember, you're not trying to sell your book – you're only looking to validate your ideas.

While speaking to your ideal reader, open up with a minute or two of light conversation to put the interviewee at ease. Buy them a drink or coffee if it's a face-to-face meeting. Then, ask them open questions related to your subject matter like:

- What are you struggling with right now?
- What would your life be like if...?
- What have you tried so far that worked/didn't work?
- What would it mean to you if...?
- Can you tell me about a time you...?

Be respectful of your interviewee's time too, and send a thank-you email or message when you're done.

I keep my reader research in a single document in Evernote. Through interviews and online research, you should be able to establish a sense of the following for your ideal reader:

- Age
- Sex
- Job
- Income
- Education
- Hopes
- Dreams
- Fears

- Frustrations

Then, while writing your book, hold in mind your ideal reader. Write to them alone. Empathise with their pains, and solve their problems. Use their language in your book. Let other authors worry about everyone else.

CRAFTING YOUR BOOK'S POSITIONING STATEMENT

By now, you should have an idea of who your ideal reader is, what they worry about and dream of. Now you're going to craft a positioning statement.

It's a succinct description of what your book is about and who it's for. A positioning statement will help you and your readers understand why your book is different from the competition and what's valuable about it. In short:

Controlling Idea + Ideal Reader = Positioning Statement

Here are three typical positioning statement templates for most popular self-help books:

- My book helps _____ who _____ get _____.
- My book teaches _____ how to _____.
- My book helps _____ who _____ achieve _____.

Now, here's my positioning statement for this book:

My book helps new writers write and sell copies of their first non-fiction book.

Writing a positioning statement for your book will help you with your book's title, sales copy, book cover and more. For example, consider the book *The 7 Habits of Highly Effective People: Powerful Lessons in Personal Change*.

It's clear from the title that this book helps people who want to overcome a personal or professional challenge. Readers should expect proven, real-world advice.

Not every author works their positioning statement directly into the title. And that's okay – but once you understand what your book is about and who it's for, you're far more likely to be able to sell it later on.

What's more, if you're self-publishing your book, you'll be able to market it in a way that attracts the attention of would-be readers. It's easier to explain who should and shouldn't buy your book if you can distill thousands of words into a single sentence.

THE SWEET SPOT

What if you don't care about your ideal reader or what's selling today on Amazon? By all means, write for yourself. Earning a living from writing doesn't equate to every writers' idea of success.

After the success of *The Catcher in the Rye*, the novelist J.D. Salinger turned away from the gaze of the public and his fans. Instead, he wrote for himself without publishing his work.

Rumour has it, upon his death, he left over two dozen completed and unpublished manuscripts in a safe in his house in New Hampshire.

You've got to admire Salinger for turning away from the public gaze. And yet, this luxury was only possible *after* the critical and commercial success of *The Catcher in the Rye*.

But what if you're not a Salinger in the making and only write what your readers want without caring if it fires you up?

Well, you'll probably get by for a while, but there are easier ways to earn a living than writing books. You'll eventually burn out.

Instead, there's a place between passion and pragmatism where you can earn a living from your craft *and* feel excited about what you're creating.

The best books appeal to their readers and the authors who write them

So position your book's ideas so they appeal to the marketplace and your creative muse.

Remember, you don't have to dominate the market or obliterate the competition to earn a decent living from your non-fiction book. Instead, find out what's keeping your ideal reader up at night and write to them with an answer that fires you up.

THE PAGES BETWEEN PASSION AND PRAGMATISM

Halbert died in his sleep in his apartment in Miami just shy of his 69th birthday. Although he wrote these letters for his son Bond, you too can apply them to write better non-fiction books

Like Halbert, find a place between passion and pragmatism. You must give your readers what they want and still feel good about sitting down to write.

Once you're there, you'll be able to make a real impact with your words and ideas... and get paid for doing it.

I believe in you and your book, good luck!

Bryan

YOUR WRITING EXERCISES

- Find three potential readers of your book and interview them for at least twenty minutes. Listen to their hopes, fears, dreams and frustrations.
- Using your research and your work from the previous chapter, craft a positioning statement for your book. Explain what it does, who it's for and why people should buy your book.

LEARNING TO EXPRESS YOURSELF FASTER

"Everything great in the world is done by neurotics; they alone founded our religions and created our masterpieces." – Marcel Proust

You dreamt of crafting pages of immaculate prose and publishing books that get more five-star reviews than you know what do to with.

You imagined your peers telling each other, "Now there's talent!" and all the while your bank balance is getting larger and larger.

And the reality?

On a good day, you sit down in Starbucks, sip your Mocha Frappuccino, nibble on a blueberry muffin, fire up Word, check your phone, email, Facebook, Twitter and Instagram... and do anything but write.

Every moment you spend with your work feels like a struggle, and what you write takes hours longer than you planned.

Even worse, when you read it, you've no idea if your work sounds reasonable or even if an alien from Mars could understand it.

Well, I've drunk the same Mocha Frappuccinos. I know many non-fiction book writers struggle to express themselves when they first try to write a book.

I CAN'T FIND MY VOICE

Before J.K. Rowling had her way, the Philosopher's Stone was a long sought-after artefact from the Middle Ages. According to legend, it could turn base metals into gold.

When they write the history of this craft, the writer's voice will stand as our Philosopher's Stone. It's an elusive entity you can spend your whole life chasing, yet never find.

I don't have it, your editor doesn't have it, and your readers certainly don't have it.

You don't set out in search of your writing voice *because you already have one*. Instead, you must develop your voice through continued and disciplined practice.

When I started writing non-fiction, I spent a lot of time trying to find my voice. I worried about writing in the first person, third person and even the second person (don't ask).

I tried to figure out how much of myself I should inject into my work and how much I should hold back. I even mimicked the style of other writers I admired.

I spent way too much time fussing about what my writing sounded like when I should have been, you know, *writing*!

HOW MARCEL PROUST CRAFTED HIS LITERARY SIX-PACK

Frenchman Marcel Proust (1871-1922) was determined to become a famous fiction writer.

His first novel, *Pleasures and Days*, was a commercial success, but Proust's critics dismissed it as all form and no substance.

They said his portrait of French society was the effort of a man who wanted to impress.

Ouch!

An unhappy Proust set out to write a more honest non-fiction work. He decided to base his work on the many stories, character sketches and lessons about psychology and life he'd collected over the years.

Proust regarded almost every setback as challenges he had to overcome. He knew what he wanted to achieve. So he committed to his idea of writing the ultimate portrait of 19th and early 20th century French society.

It took Proust more than 18 years to finish the eighteen volumes of *In Search of Lost Time*, and that's to say nothing of the research beforehand.

Today, that book is one the 20th century's most respected non-fiction books.

Proust overcame failure, he stopped trying to impress, and he developed his writing voice.

He said:

> When you work to please others you can't succeed, but the things you do to satisfy yourself stand a chance of catching someone's interest.

Proust developed his writing through consistent practice, and he crafted the writer's equivalent of a six-pack.

DEVELOPING YOUR WRITER'S SIX-PACK

Let's say you spent six months eating Häagen-Dazs and watching reruns of *Keeping Up with the Kardashians*.

Then one day, you get up, go to the gym and try to bench-press your bodyweight.

What would happen next?

A small coronary event perhaps.

Even if you're not inclined towards reality television or chocolate ice cream, any gym coach worth their protein shakes will say:

You must gradually increase the amount of weights you lift each session.

While in my early twenties, my career as a journalist came to a depressing halt. To pay the mounting bills, I found a job as a careworker for people with intellectual disabilities.

I struggled to find some time outside of work to write every day.

I told myself the blank page would keep until tomorrow and that I could write at the weekend. I even tried looking at myself in the mirror and telling myself, *Don't be lazy, just work harder.*

When I finally had the guts to sit down in front of the blank page and write, I could barely remember where I left off or what I wanted to say.

It took me so long to find the right words that each time I wrote, I felt like a beginner. I only learnt to write by showing up consistently and increasing how long I spent writing gradually.

You must progress towards your goal of writing a book day-by-day. You must develop your literary chops.

'But I'm a writer, not a weight lifter.'

I get it... but you'll learn to express yourself through measured progress.

For today, write just 300 words. Tomorrow, write 350 words. The day after that, write 400 words. Keep going until you can write 1,000 or even 2,000 words in a single session.

What if word counts aren't your thing?

Practice sitting down and writing for 15 minutes today, 20 minutes tomorrow and so on. Do this until writing for an hour or two each day becomes a habit.

Showing up consistently each day will help you express yourself. It's the secret to developing your writing voice. From there, you can capture the attention of new readers.

USE EVERYTHING

Proust spent much of his young life reading books, going on long walks and writing letters He loved frolicking at aristocratic French parties, and he didn't care for accomplishments. His friends and even Proust himself bemoaned the time he was wasting.

How wrong they were.

Proust applied or used almost every lesson he learnt from these activities, and he included these lessons in *In Search of Lost Time*.

Proust used everything for his greatest work. When Proust wanted to write about plants and flowers, he drove into the countryside and studied them for hours.

When Proust wanted to create a character like a wealthy debutante for his work, he found her equivalent in French society.

Then, he got himself invited to the same events she attended. He even went as far as gathering his friends for a dinner party where he studied them intensely and recorded what they said.

Yes, Proust's approach was extreme, but you should try and use everything too.

Consider the topics you're passionate about and always ask yourself if what you're writing fires you up. Dive deeper into your genre. Dive beyond superficial reading online or a simple Google search.

Read often and outside of your comfort zone. Mine your personal life for relevant stories and anecdotes. Consider the last thing you learnt and what you can say that no one else can. Be outrageous. Take a bloody stance.

Put it all in.

(Later on, you can edit your writing and take out the bits that don't work or where you've said too much).

PLOTTERS VS. PANTSERS

Okay, so you're ready to take a stance and do the work – what now?

Well, most people think there are two types of writers: rich ones... and the rest of us. Dig a little deeper, and you'll find out there are also pantsers and plotters.

Pantsers are writers who sit down in front of the blank page with only a vague idea of where they are going or what they want to write a book about.

They write from the seat of their pants, inventing things as they go along, and they are happy to see where their ideas and research take them.

They write with a connection to God, their muse or their subconscious. More often than not, *they write fiction or literary non-fiction.*

Proust's writing is exploratory, and it has all the hallmarks of a pantser. The American essayist Henry Miller was probably a pantser too, as he approached his literary essays like a "voyage of discover".

Plotters, on the other hand, spend weeks or months organising their ideas and deciding what they want to write about in advance.

When plotters sit down to work, they have a strong idea of what they're going to say, and they have the research to back it up.

Robert Greene, the author of *Mastery, The Art of Seduction* and *The 48 Laws of Power*, is a plotter.

Those non-fiction books are a curious blend of psychology, history and self-help. They've also sold millions of copies, and *The 48 Laws of Power* is particularly popular in US prisons.

Greene says he typically reads an eye-watering 300 to 400 books about a particular topic before he starts "typing up" his books.

He spends hundreds of hours reading and researching, taking care to organise his ideas on a series of annotated 4x6-inch index cards.

Greene colour-codes these cards based on categories or themes and files them in a box. He sorts through his research regularly, finding great value in bumping up against old ideas while working on new ones.

In a Reddit AMA, Greene says about this trusted system:

> I read a book, very carefully, writing on the margins with all kinds of notes. A few weeks later I return to the book, and transfer my scribbles on to note cards, each card representing an important theme in the book.

Malcolm Gladwell combines elements of both approaches.

He interviews subjects extensively for his books before he starts writing. However, he cautions against making up one's mind until the research is complete:

> I would say that probably half of the interviews I do end up on the

cutting room floor–or, at least, are used in later articles. The purpose of research is to cast as wide a net as possible. I tend to start researching something with only the vaguest idea in mind of where I want to end up. It's a mistake to make up your mind too soon.

FINDING OUT WHAT KIND OF WRITER YOU ARE

I've tried plotting and writing from the seat of my pants. After years of painful rewrites, unfinished manuscripts and pulling my hair out, I found out I'm a plotter.

I need to know what I'm writing about in advance. Being a plotter enables struggling non-fiction writers to finish their books faster.

Being a pantser is more useful for fiction writers and literary non-fiction writers.

That said, there are no hard-and-fast rules. You'll discover what kind of writer you are if you put down the Häagen-Dazs and turn up in front of the blank page.

GET READY TO CRUSH IT LIKE MARCEL PROUST

Proust saw expressing himself through writing as a lifelong pursuit. He finished his 18-volume memoir just two days before he died, and he never saw the final version of his masterpiece in print.

I'm not suggesting you write on your deathbed, but doing the work often means going at it longer and harder than what feels like normal. It means practising expressing yourself day after day – every day.

If you're struggling, find a great book that you enjoy reading. Then pick a paragraph, page or chapter from this book and write it out by hand.

No, don't type it!

Handwriting a piece you like will help you draw upon the author's style and approach. I know it may feel inefficient, but sometimes new writers need to slow down.

This practice will enable you to figure out how successful writers tell stories and organise their ideas. Besides, there's plenty of time for efficient and productive writing later on.

Like the weight lifter who finally crushes it in the gym, you'll improve your craft through consistent practice.

Anything else is just Häagen-Dazs.

YOUR WRITING EXERCISES

- Are you a plotter or a pantser? The only way to find out is to start writing and test both approaches.
- Lift your literary weights by writing for 30 minutes or by producing 300 words today. Then increase your output gradually, because today's pain is tomorrow's gain.

TAKING CHARGE OF YOUR TOOLS
BEFORE THEY TAKE CHARGE OF YOU

"The big artist keeps an eye on nature and steals her tools."– Thomas Eakins

Should you write your book on a computer, by hand or with that gold Montblanc pen that you break out for special occasions?

What killer writing application do six-figure authors use?

And *just when* is your pencil sharp enough?

Of course, many aspiring authors wonder if they should write their book with pen and paper or if they need the perfect writing app to get going.

Well, there's a time and place for both types of tools.

GOING ANALOGUE

Marcel Proust, Leo Tolstoy and W. B. Yeats did just fine without a computer or access to the internet.

There's something refreshing about a good notebook. You don't have to upgrade, refresh or recharge it. You don't have to worry about index cards freezing or not syncing properly.

A whiteboard will never prompt you for your password, need to be reset or have trouble connecting to your WiFi.

Science is on the side of analogue tools too.

Here's what top psychologists Pam A. Mueller of Princeton and Daniel M. Oppenheimer of the University of California found:

They discovered that students learn better when they take notes by hand rather than when typing on a keyboard. They wrote:

> ...whereas taking more notes can be beneficial, laptop note takers' tendency to transcribe lectures verbatim rather than processing information and reframing it in their own words is detrimental to learning.

Now you may not be studying for an exam, but writing by hand could help you produce a better book.

So file your notes, wipe down your desk, pair your pencils and fill your pens. Or if you're editing your book, print out early drafts, and read through your manuscript and mark it up with a red pen while standing up.

If it pains you to sit at a desk, take a pen and a notebook and go to your local coffee shop or into nature.

I love the writing practice of copying out other people's works by hand. I take a chapter from a book I like or a piece of writing by an author I admire, and I write it out.

Longhand writing is slower and more meditative than anything I achieve with a digital tool. And yet, this practice helps me to learn more of other authors' writing styles. It's also useful if you feel blocked or uninspired by your book.

If you get distracted while using analogue tools, take a note from William Faulkner.

He removed the doorknob from his door and brought it into his study to prevent people from intruding and distracting him while he wrote. (At the very least, you could unplug your modem and turn off your phone.)

When I'm blocked, I turn off my computer, disconnect from the grid and write a rough draft (or an outline) in a notebook or A4 or letter paper pad. There's nothing to update, backup, search or check. All I can do is write.

When to Use Analogue Writing Tools

- For capturing ideas on the go
- When you keep getting distracted
- For getting a messy first draft out of your head
- When you're blocked or uninspired
- For practising your craft
- When you want to create a rough outline of your book

GOING DIGITAL

Although I use analogue writing tools, I always find my way back to a digital writing tool once I'm unstuck. I break out in cold sweats when I think about losing a paper copy of a first draft (or even an outline).

Besides, publishing the contents of a tattered Moleskine notebook is unpractical.

I capture ideas on the go and store them in Evernote. Later, I write book chapters like this one using Scrivener. The latter is ideal for managing complicated and even multiple writing projects.

Yes, there's a small learning curve, but you'll save hours of time editing your book. For example, you can organise the chapters or sections of any book using a drag-and-drop interface. That's a lot faster than manipulating large blocks of text in Word or playing around with multiple files on your machine.

The Scrivener Binder: Here you can drag and drop individual book chapters

Scrivener also features several powerful in-built editing tools. My favourites include:

- Digital index cards (more on those later)
- Target word counts for individual chapters
- A custom status option for each chapter
- The ability to work on chapters side-by-side
- A progress bar for individual chapters

For example, I use the custom status in Scrivener to mark chapters as "Done", "Not done", "Ready for an editor" and so on. This helps me track what I need to write next.

THE ART OF WRITING A NON-FICTION BOOK

Notice the custom status for each chapter

When I finish a manuscript, I export it from Scrivener, and I lay it out using the self-publishing tool Vellum.

This tool helps me prepare the book file for uploading to stores like Amazon. Before using Vellum, I paid designers to do this for me. Later, I'll cover self-publishing a non-fiction book in detail.

When to Use Digital Writing Tools

- For organising your ideas and research
- When you're ready to write a more polished draft of your book
- For editing your book
- For preparing your book for publication
- For marketing and selling your work

MASTERING DICTATION

Several years ago, I struggled with repetitive strain injury, or RSI. Spending hours hunched over a keyboard for a day job and then again at night wasn't good for my fingers.

One day, I spent two hours transcribing an interview by hand. When I got home, I filled a sink with ice-cold water and plunged my aching hands into it for relief.

I overcame RSI by buying a special mouse and also by using a mouse mat and keyboard with wrist guards.

That eased my RSI for a time, but mastering dictation helped too.

Dictation software, like Dragon Dictate and Dragon Naturally Speaking, is easier to learn and more accurate than ever.

If you suffer from RSI or get pain in your fingers from typing, dictation is ideal. You can dictate your book while standing, walking around the room or even without using your hands.

I can type about a five hundred to thousand words in 30 minutes if I know what I'm writing about. On the other hand, I can dictate up to 3,000 to 4,000 words in 30 minutes.

Dictation is also ideal for writing first drafts. Matthew Weiner, the showrunner of *Mad Men*, recently revealed he hired a transcriber to record his thoughts for early drafts of his hit show:

> I paid people to do research, inundated myself with material, and even hired a writer's assistant to dictate to because I was too tired to type. (It also freed my imagination).

The job of any first draft is to exist. With dictation, it's harder to edit and write at the same time. You're more likely to hit your daily target word count and get a messy first draft out of your head and onto the blank page.

Dictation helps you focus too. It's harder to stop dictating because you want to check your email, browse Facebook or do something that has nothing to do with writing.

It also encourages conversational types of writing. Because I'm speaking and not typing, I'm less likely to use bigger words or turn to complicated language and turns of phrase.

Arguably, dictation holds less value for literary non-fiction writers. It's not ideal for experimenting with your sentences or playing around with words either.

HOW TO DICTATE YOUR BOOK

The poet, teacher and non-fiction author Natalie Goldberg tells new writers to "keep your hand moving."

When it comes to dictation, keep your mouth moving!

You'll need to dictate in a quiet room with the right equipment. The quality of your microphone and environment directs the accuracy of your software.

I first tried using the inbuilt microphone on my computer for dictation, but my accuracy was below 50%. Then I tried using a cheap headset I had in my wardrobe. That didn't improve the quality much either.

So I spent around $100 on a professional dictation headset and that dramatically improved my accuracy.

If you haven't dictated a book before, it'll take time to learn this new skill so don't expect a dramatic increase in your word count... at least at first.

As with acquiring any new writing skill, allow time for a learning curve. It took me some trial and error to figure out how to build dictation into my writing workflow.

For example, you will have to learn how to speak punctuation commands. So when I want a full stop, I have to say the words "full stop." When I want to start a new paragraph, I have to say "new paragraph."

And so on.

You'll also have to avoid using filler words like "you know."

Don't expect 100% accuracy.

This will improve as the software adapts to your voice. However, it won't recognise every word you say, particularly technical terms and words affected by your accent.

For instance, my daughter has a traditional Irish name. No matter how many times I tried, I couldn't train the dictation software I use to recognise her name. I tried spelling the name and using various other tips and tricks, but the software still insisted on mangling it.

So now whenever I'm dictating a journal entry and I want to use her name, I speak a placeholder word Dragon Dictate recognises.

In this case, I'll use the name "Sarah", or I call her "my daughter." Then when I'm editing the journal entry, I search for the word 'Sarah' and replace it with my daughter's name.

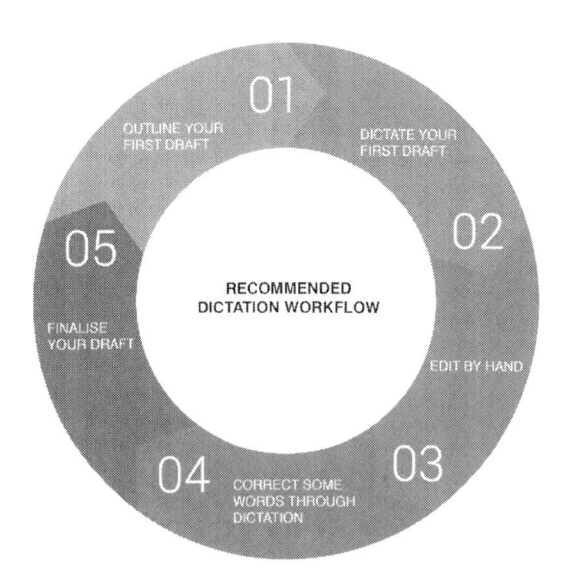

RECOMMENDED DICTATION WORKFLOW

01 OUTLINE YOUR FIRST DRAFT
02 DICTATE YOUR FIRST DRAFT
03 EDIT BY HAND
04 CORRECT SOME WORDS THROUGH DICTATION
05 FINALISE YOUR DRAFT

Tips for Dictating Your Book

- Before investing in expensive software or a microphone, experiment with the dictation software built into Windows/OSX or Google Docs.
- When you're ready, use a microphone purpose-built for dictation.

- If you're using Dragon Dictate or Dragon Naturally Speaking, teach the software using your writing, rather than completing the built-in training. This approach will improve your accuracy.
- Speak in complete sentences, and speak your punctuation.
- Keep your chapter outline next to where you dictate, so you know what you're about to say next.
- Use filler words for complicated terms dictation software gets wrong.
- Write early drafts using dictation software; edit later drafts using your keyboard.

OWNING YOUR TOOLS

Today's digital writing tools may be powerful, but (if you're like me) you can spend more time looking for the perfect setup than writing. Only use as many digital tools as you need. Your time is better spent improving your craft and building relationships with readers.

Your writing tools of choice should support your writing, and you should own them rather than letting them own you.

How?

Turn off all the notifications on your computer so you're not dragged into another application while writing. Then close everything except your writing application of choice.

If you're getting distracted by viral cat videos, disconnect from the grid. I know one writer who even plugs out her modem while working on her book and stashes it in the attic.

Do whatever it takes, write with whatever you want, wherever you want, as long as you can finish your drafts.

GETTING THE JOB DONE

Many writers use analogue tools at some point. American non-fiction author Robert Greene, for example, uses index cards to outline his books before writing them. Digital tools, too, can save you a lot of time and help you connect with readers.

Knowing when to go analogue and digital is a useful writing skill to build. That said, always remember, your craft and readers come before any new tool.

In his book *Tribes*, Seth Godin writes:

> The tactics are irrelevant, and the technology will always be changing. The essential lesson is that every day it gets easier to tighten the relationships you have with the people who choose to follow you.

So spend most of your time working on your drafts. Concentrate on improving your craft. And then build relationships with your readers.

YOUR WRITING EXERCISES

- After you've finished the day's writing, set aside a little time for learning a new tool. Sure, there's a small learning curve to mastering Scrivener and even dictation, but you could save hours later on.
- The next time you feel blocked or when your word count plummets, take out a notepad and write out a passage by your favourite writer.

KNOWING WHEN IT'S TIME TO WRITE (AND FINDING SPACE TO DO IT)

"Tell me, what is it you plan to do with your one wild and precious life?" – Mary Oliver

I spent a year working as a copywriter in a large, air-conditioned office half an hour outside Dublin. I wrote alongside 100 other people, almost none of whom were writers.

One Monday, my boss asked me to produce a 3,000-word guide about the advantages of using cloud-based software, and he gave me a deadline to sweat over.

It didn't help that the topic was drier than a gin and tonic. I trudged through the first 200 words of an early draft, hoping I'd submit the piece on time.

While writing, I didn't pay much attention to the dull sound of my co-worker Jackie's voice or to what she was saying... at first.

While I clacked away on my keyboard, she stood:

"But you told me our deposit for the house was good and that we'd have the keys by the summer. I can't wait until September."

"Jackie, you must be patient," the estate agency said.

"I've been patient for months," Jackie shouted into her phone. "This isn't good enough. You're full of it."

Jackie berated her estate agent for five minutes before walking out of the office and slamming the door behind her.

I tried to focus on what I was writing, but all I could think about was the time I bought a house with my wife and how I hated the entire process. We'd argued for weeks about which one to buy. I didn't envy what Jackie was going through or her estate agent.

What did Jackie's real estate agent think of her? And what did any of this have to do with cloud-based software?

Ten minutes later, Jackie sat down at her desk, looked at me and said, "Don't ask."

She produced a Granny Smith apple, a bottle of Coca-Cola and packet of salt and vinegar crisps from the recesses of her brown leather handbag.

I put my fingers on the keyboard and tried to type, but then Jackie began to bite into her apple and crisps.

Crunch. Crunch. Crunch.

Jackie only stopped eating to sigh, swear under her breath and tap out a message on her phone.

I'd type and then... *Crunch. Crunch. Crunch.*

When five o'clock rolled around, I'd only written 150 words.

The next morning, my manager asked about the guide.

"It's going well," I said, thinking of the 2,850 words I still had to wade though.

"When can I expect a draft to review?" he said.

"It'll be on time," I said. "Don't worry."

I didn't want to tell him how behind I was. I needed this job to work out, and Jackie's real estate problems weren't helping.

So I took my laptop and notes and locked myself alone into a small room at the back of the office, a room devoid of apples, crisps and Jackie. I forced myself to sit in the chair, and I wrote for three hours until I finished a workable draft.

After lunch, I sat back at my desk and emailed a draft to my boss.

"Where were you Bryan?" Jackie asked.

"I was in a meeting," I said. "And it lasted all morning. How's your house coming on?"

ASSOCIATE ONE PLACE WITH WRITING

If you're having trouble finding time or space for your book, don't give up. I don't doubt your commitment, and you're not alone. Before writing this chapter, I read an email from one new writer who said:

> What I get from my wife is lip service (which would be OK if she'd let me kiss her once in a while). She knows my desire to be an author. She tells others how much time I spend writing in a way that makes me believe she's behind me. Then, like the other day...she tells me...she has something more important for me to do.

Now, instead of paying lip service to your book, take a note from Virginia Woolf. She wrote:

> A woman must have money and a room of her own if she is to write fiction.

Woolf was referring to a woman's ability to support herself and her writing financially. And yet, even today, male and female writers need a warm and quiet place with a desk, a chair and a computer or a pen and notepad.

It's up to you to seek out the quietness and space you need to write your book. Going to a room to work alone may look strange to others, but take heart: you're putting your book first.

These days, I write in a small room at the top of my house. I have a sunlight lamp, a mic for dictation and a set of noise-cancelling headphones. This setup enables me to enter a bubble. I can concentrate on writing that first draft without worrying about the logistics of writing.

When I'm feeling blocked, I go for a long walk and dictate to my phone, or I go to a coffee shop and bang out the first draft over an Americano.

You could carve out a quiet space in your house, in a coffee shop, the local library or your car. The 'where' doesn't matter as much as having that space, where you write consistently.

When the short story writer and poet Raymond Carver was starting off, he often wrote his drafts alone in his car. He told the *Paris Review*:

> I used to go out and sit in the car and try to write something on a pad on my knee.

Associate a place with writing and little else, and you'll slip into your creative groove more easily.

If it's somewhere public, just remember to leave a tip.

YOUR BULLET-PROOF GUIDE TO CREATING AN EARLY MORNING WRITING ROUTINE

For years, I wrote late at night, after the kids went to bed.

Then I'd struggle to get up the following day, go to work and spend time with the kids. It was all I could do not to pry my eyelids open with matchsticks.

Inevitably, I wrote less.

Putting writing last meant it was least likely to happen.

Then I discovered science is on the side of early morning writing. The American philosopher and psychologist William James said:

> The great thing, then, in all education, is to make automatic and habitual, as early as possible, as many useful actions as we can, and to guard against the growing into ways that are likely to be disadvantageous to us, as we should guard against the plague.

Famous early morning artists include the composer Ludwig van

Beethoven, the Danish philosopher Søren Kierkegaard and American author Ernest Hemingway.

My writing routine starts with climbing out of my pit sometime between 5.30 and 6.15 a.m.

I wash my face with cold water, meditate for 20 minutes and brew a strong coffee sweetened with honey.

Then I record five to ten ideas on paper or in Evernote. This act helps me warm up before writing for 60 to 90 minutes. My morning routine ends around 8 a.m. when it's time to get the kids up for school. Now, my writing routine works for me, but yours will look different.

Ask yourself what your ideal morning routine looks like, and write it down on paper. Thinking it through will help you find more time for working on your non-fiction book.

DECIDE WHEN TO GET UP

Pick your target time for getting up, and work slowly towards this time. Don't be a hero. If you set your alarm clock for 4 a.m. tomorrow morning, you may get up, but you'll feel exhausted. You're also unlikely to repeat this heroic feat of endurance.

Instead, set your alarm clock for half an hour earlier than your regular rising time. On the following day, set your alarm for 45 minutes earlier.

And so on.

If I rise any earlier than 5.30 a.m., I'm too exhausted to function during the day. If I rise any later than 6.15 a.m., I don't have enough time to write before life arrives. My target rising time gives me a 45-minute window between 5.30 a.m. and 6.15 a.m.

If you want to create an early morning writing routine, find enough time to write without interruption before the day begins. But don't get up so early that you risk falling asleep on your keyboard.

... AND WHEN TO SLEEP

Before you go to bed, write a note to yourself about what chapter you're going to work on. Then open up your writing application and arrange your notes.

These small acts prime your subconscious to wrestle with your book even while you're sleeping.

Each night, I prepare the following day's writing. I tidy up where I work, and I leave a short note to myself.

It says things like "fix the damn conclusion" or "work viral cat videos into chapter nine."

Setting an alarm clock for going to bed helps too. This act may sound bizarre, but you probably set one for getting up, so consider it a mindset shift.

When it rings, stop checking your emails, using your computer, playing with your phone or doing anything else that keeps you up.

Before you go to bed, put your alarm in a different room from where you sleep.

When it rings, you'll have to get out of bed and go into the other room to turn it off. The act of moving complicates pressing the snooze button or rolling over and going back to sleep.

Finally, if your partner goes to bed later than you, consider using earplugs or an eye mask.

WHAT YOU GET FOR RISING EARLY

One evening over a beer, I explained my early morning writing habit to a friend.

"When you get up before everyone else, you give the best of yourself to yourself," I said.

My friend almost choked on his beer.

"You're crazy," he said, laughing. "Where do you get this stuff from?"

My friend isn't a writer, and I couldn't expect him to understand it's the job of a writer to sit alone in a quiet room and work for hours at a time.

If the demands of your job leave you physically or mentally exhausted, you're less likely to sit down and write. What's more, when you do, the quality of your writing will suffer.

Like a lot of writers, I doubled my weekly word count by rising early to work on my book.

When you get up early in the morning, you're at your peak. No matter what happens during the day, you'll already be ahead because you've worked on your book.

BUT I REALLY AM A NIGHT PERSON!

I don't get up early every day. I sleep late at least one day on the weekend, and some days it's not possible or practical to get up early because of the demands of the previous day.

I accept these days as times to rest instead of seeing them as setbacks that prevent me from finishing a book.

I'm not going to lie and say I find time to write 365 days a year either, but when I write, I feel lighter. When I write first thing, even if it's just a journal entry, I don't come home after an exhausting day and think:

Oh no, I still have to sit down in front of the computer and fill a blank page.

If the demands of daily life aren't intruding, by all means, work on your book during the afternoon or at night. Every writer is different.

The most important thing is turning up in front of the blank page consistently and being able to work without interruption.

KEEPING UP WITH THE PROFESSIONALS

These days, I rarely have to deal with unreliable estate agents, crunchy apples and noisy packets of crisps. And yet, working alone presents a different set of challenges.

No matter where I write, I'm still free to put things off, procrastinate and say it will keep till later. I've often woken up, checked email, phoned the cable company about my bill, cleaned up after the dog and done everything else but write 500 to 1,000 words.

It took me years to learn writing is one of the most important things I need to do each day, and it's my job to minimise interruptions.

Before email.

Before social media.

Before the news.

And sometimes even before breakfast.

Remember, a doctor doesn't look at their scalpel and wonder if they'll operate now or when *Keeping Up with the Kardashians* is over.

They do their work because they are professionals.

So pick a time for working on your book every day, block-book it in your calendar and keep your appointment. Like pennies filling a jar, these writing sessions will accumulate in value over time.

One day, you'll stop typing, see you finished a 2,000 word chapter in one session and wonder, "How did I get here?"

YOUR WRITING EXERCISES

- Dedicate one place in your house, apartment or where you live to working on your book, and go there each day.
- Expect life to get in the way. When it does, pour it a glass of wine, listen to its problems and, when it passes out on the couch, get back to work.

PART II
WRITING YOUR NON-FICTION BOOK

FINDING MORE IDEAS THAN YOU KNOW WHAT TO DO WITH

"I think like a genius, I write like a distinguished author, and I speak like a child." – Vladimir Nabokov

The Stradivarius violin has an unparalleled reputation for tone and clarity, and a single instrument is worth up to $16 million. Now, that's a lot of money to pay for a violin, so why is it so lust-worthy?

Italian craftsman Antonio Stradivari created these violins from wood affected by a mini-Ice Age during the 1700s.

Only 600 of these Italian violins exist today... and it's impossible to replicate them. Recently, a team of Dutch scientists led by Dr. Berend Stoel scanned five of these instruments and compared them to modern violins.

Dr. Stoel said:

> It could be a difference in climate when the trees were harvested, or it could also be that the masters used some secret treatment on the wood, or it could be that over the course of three hundred years the violins just get better in tone.

What does this talk about violins have to do with finding ideas for your non-fiction book? Well, you need great materials if you want to create your masterpiece.

Hell, you need good materials if you're going to write something that sells.

By materials, I don't mean a pot of ink and a golden pen with a twelve-inch pink feather dangling off the end. I'm talking about the kinds of ideas that are everywhere and that you can use to write a great book... if you know where to look.

I WROTE WITH LOUSY MATERIALS... AND THIS IS WHAT HAPPENED

Confession: when I was a fresh-faced freelance journalist in my early twenties, I didn't care for research or finding ideas.

I spent days sitting on my ass waiting for my editor to send me a commission when I should have been on the lookout for ideas and news stories.

I'm a writer... I don't have time for research.

I thought writing meant pressing my fingers against the keyboard. I believed 'doing the work' meant filling the screen with random musings about what it's like to have a quarter-life crisis.

Picking up the phone and talking to living, breathing people felt like a distraction from putting one word after another on the blank page. I should have listened to Truman Capote, who said, "That's not writing, that's typing."

If I sound like I was a hard-working (if misguided) freelance journalist, don't let me fool you.

I had enough time to sit in front of the computer screen in my underwear, pick at half-eaten chocolate bars, drink cold tea and play *World of Warcraft* until 3.23 a.m.

Who has time to interview people or read through old books when you could be going on a four-hour dungeon raid?

I didn't bother looking for materials and ideas for my writing, and suffice to say, my editors didn't call with new commissions.

So, classmates from college landed jobs with national newspapers and with radio stations, while I languished on the sidelines, wondering what I'd done wrong.

After a stint on the unemployment line, I quit on journalism, but I didn't quit on writing. I looked at successful authors and wondered: *Where do they find their ideas?*

Here's what I discovered:

PROFESSIONAL AUTHORS ARE ALWAYS LOOKING FOR IDEAS

I know a smart freelance writer who keeps a **future file** of news stories and other articles that she has worked on or read. She returns to these articles every few months to write an updated version. Her editors love it.

Who plans that far ahead?

Freelance writers who earn six figures a year, that's who, and it's a strategy I wish I'd known about before I handed back my press pass.

Even Thomas Jefferson jotted down notes about everything from the growth of plants and flowers to observations about daily life.

But I'm a storyteller, why should I care about future files and swipe files?

Well, if you wait for inspiration to arrive, you'll be stood up.

From the age of 19, Mark Twain carried a personal pocket notebook with him and recorded his observations. The novelist John Cheever kept a journal throughout his life, and he often left entries about stories he was writing or wanted to write.

George Lucas also keeps a notebook with him when he's shooting a film.

Perhaps he should have carried around that notebook a little longer while writing the prequels, but you can't deny his creativity.

WHATEVER YOU WRITE, YOU'RE A COLLECTOR OF IDEAS.

Perhaps you collect stories from your personal life in a journal?

Here's one I found:

One time, my two-year-old daughter jammed a pink crayon up her nose, and I had to buy a pair of tweezers to take it out.

Perhaps you collect small details from your day?

And another:

One time, I was waiting outside a gym to collect my wife from her class. A shaven-headed bodybuilder walked outside, opened a pack of cooked chicken fillets and ate them one by one.

Or perhaps you collect random information from magazines you read?

And one more:

There's a funny type of violin from years past. It's made of whiskey water and a special wood, and it costs millions of dollars.

You may know what to do with these stories today or even tomorrow, but it's all material.

FINDING CREATIVE IDEAS THROUGH READING

I've always loved to read, but when I was a budding journalist, I preferred reading fiction I enjoyed. I didn't spend much time reading non-fiction books outside my comfort zone.

Now, that might be okay for somebody whose career doesn't involve words and ideas, but it's poison for an ASPIRING PROFESSIONAL AUTHOR.

If you're writing a non-fiction book, then reading is part of your job. You must read outside of your comfort zone. You must include the work of writers you admire and writers you detest, all while taking notes and writing ideas and your opinions down.

If you fail to feed your mind, don't expect it to serve you quality ideas when you sit down in front of the blank page.

YOU NEED MORE BUTTERFLIES IN YOUR LIFE

Lots of writers use their curious side-interests and hobbies for their works.

The British author Virginia Woolf chronicled her long walks around her neighbourhood in her journals and essays.

Henry David Thoreau moved to the woodlands near Walden Pond in Massachusetts for two years, where he wrote about his self-imposed exile.

The American essayist and novelist John Cheever wrote about swimming, cycling and his extracurricular activities:

> I do have trouble with the dead hours of the afternoon without skating, skiing, bicycling, swimming, or sexual discharges or drink.

Now, Cheever liked to fill a glass or take off his pants to pass the time, but if you're struggling to find ideas, put your book and pen (or your partner) down.

Go for a short walk, work out in the gym or do something strenuous. The flow of blood and change of environment will kickstart your brain in intriguing directions.

Think of yourself as like the Danish philosopher Søren Kierkegaard. He wrote early in the morning before setting off for an afternoon walk around Copenhagen. Then he returned to write in the evening.

Charles Dickens was another prolific walker you could aspire to. On a given day, Dickens walked 12 or more miles around Kent or through the streets of Victorian London.

He used many moments from these walks as inspiration for his novels. In *Charles Dickens: A Critical Study*, critic G.K. Chesterton writes:

> There are details in Dickens' descriptions – a window, or a railing, or the keyhole of a door – which he endows with demoniac life. The things seem more actual than things really are.

Even if you don't think of an idea while exercising, you will have more energy for tackling your creative problem.

The ever-humble Russian writer Vladimir Nabokov fed his writing with one of the stranger hobbies I've come across. He had little time for eating, socialising or drinking coffee with friends.

Instead he loved to solve chess problems and study butterflies. Both interests informed his work; his novel *Zashchita Luzhina* (*The Luzhin Defense*), features an insane chess player.

Nabokov writes in his memoir:

> And the highest enjoyment of timelessness...is when I stand among rare butterflies and their food plants. This is ecstasy, and behind the ecstasy is something else, which is hard to explain. It is like a momentary vacuum into which rushes all that I love.

THE CASE FOR TAKING A BREAK

One Sunday afternoon last July, I spent two hours trying to write a chapter for my last book. Getting nowhere and being all out of ideas, I put on a pair of trainers and went for a run.

I was ten km in and half-way around the local park when I thought of a breakthrough.

Covered in mud, I stopped running, pulled out my phone and opened the voice memo app.

I was standing in a puddle with water up to my ankles, soaked in sweat and roaring into my phone about 'needing more butterflies' in my life, when a 72-year-old lady and her manicured white poodle walked around the corner.

She mouthed 'morning' and hurried along with her dog.

When I got home that evening, I wrote for two hours without interruption; that woman and her judgmental poodle be damned.

So the next time you feel stuck or uninspired, read, pick up the phone, interview someone, go for a walk with your poodle or chase rare butterflies... no matter what kind of writer you are, your side-interests will help you reignite your creative spark.

Every time you do this, you'll learn more about how your creative process works and where the best ideas for your book come from.

HOW TO CAPTURE YOUR CREATIVE IDEAS

Keep a **swipe file** where you store facts, figures, headlines and ads relating to your area of interest or book.

You could swipe headlines and first lines, inspiring videos and pictures and compelling emails. Your file is a repository of information that, if it's not relevant to your book, will be of use at some point. Pinterest, for example, is a social swipe file.

Copywriters and advertisers keep ideas and research in their swipe files.

Famous copywriter Gary Halbert wrote a letter from prison telling his son to keep a swipe file up to date with "hot new ideas, good layouts, unusual propositions and so on."

You can also take notes using digital tools, like an app on your smartphone, or by using a small notebook that fits in your pocket.

I like using the tool Evernote. It acts as my digital brain and enables me to tag each idea. I save interesting articles, research, quotes, thoughts about books, anecdotes and more into this software. I also categorise the notes by project and type.

When I was researching my last book, *The Power of Creativity*, for example, I used the tag 'creativity' for relevant notes and ideas I wanted to find later on.

You don't have to use Evernote or worry about painful categorisation methods. Use the note-taking app on your phone, record audio files with a memo app or turn to a simple plain text editor.

Don't obsess about going digital.

Halbert got by without his digital brain. Write your ideas down on the back of your hand if you must. When I do this in public, people look at me funny.

There's that weird guy who looks off into the distance and then scribbles on the back of his hand.

If this happens to you, pay no attention to these misguided fools!

You don't want to sit down in front of the computer and realise "Baby, I've got nothing."

WHAT TO DO WITH GREAT MATERIALS

I can't promise your book will sell for $16 million in three hundred years' time. I also don't have any ancient water from a church to offer unless you count whisky.

Even if I could offer you a secret ingredient for finding amazing ideas, there's no guarantee you'll produce a masterpiece. Dr. Stoel and his team offer this caveat:

> If you are a lousy violin maker and use the best wood, you will still end up with a very bad violin.

The same applies to writing a non-fiction book.

If you're a lousy writer, all the best ideas in the world aren't much use to you. You have to take time to organise your ideas, gain the writing skills you need and then express yourself.

Then, you'll stand a better chance of finding readers and earning a living from your writing. And that's what we'll cover throughout this book.

YOUR WRITING EXERCISES

- If you're feeling blocked or devoid of ideas, fill up with someone else's ideas.
- Go for a walk/run/swim or climb your personal Everest, because exercise is fuel for finding inspiration.

RESEARCHING YOUR BOOK: THE NOBEL PRIZE APPROACH

"Study hard what interests you the most in the most undisciplined, irreverent and original manner possible." – Richard Feynman

Richard Feynman (1918-1988) was a top US scientist (and a renowned bongo player). After WWII, he spent almost a year teaching science in Rio de Janeiro. He went to Brazil as part of a programme sponsored by the US government to instruct would-be teachers.

During WWII, Feynman helped his country build the atomic bomb, but he faced a different set of problems in Brazil.

The Brazilian elementary students' habit of buying and reading physics books impressed Feynman. And yet he couldn't understand why the country produced so few physicists.

His college students perplexed him too. When he asked them specific questions, they answered correctly almost immediately.

When Feynman asked a follow-up question or asked the same question while teaching a related topic, his students looked at him like he was speaking Swahili. After some digging, Feynman discovered his students had memorised their textbooks line by line.

They were able to recite basic physics laws like, "Light is reflected from a medium with an index," but they had no idea as to *the why* behind these laws.

One day in an engineering lecture, Feynman watched students write down what the lecturer said, verbatim.

He asked one student what he was doing.

And the student replied: "Oh, we study them. We'll have an exam."

To this student and many others, mastery of a topic meant memorisation.

Feynman gave a lecture at the end of his trip and told students and faculty, "No science is being taught in Brazil."

He picked a page at random from a physics book and read out a definition of triboluminescence. This concept describes the emission of light from a substance caused by rubbing and so on.

Feynman explained anyone could read this definition aloud, but that wasn't enough. He told the perplexed group of attendees:

> And there, have you got science? No! You have only told about what a word means in terms of other words. You haven't told anything about nature–what crystals produce light when you crush them, why they produce light. Did any students go home and *try it*? He can't.

Feynman argued the Brazilian system was denying his students a useful college education. He claimed students were passing exams and teaching others how to pass exams, without understanding what they'd memorised.

When it comes to what you're teaching or writing about, I wouldn't want you to deny yourself or your readers a useful experience. So ask yourself, *'Do I understand what I'm writing about?'*

It's not enough to simply plop down what you found on the blank page like a toddler does his dinner and tell the reader, "Here, look!"

It's your job to immerse yourself in a topic through deep reading and then bring back what you find for your readers.

THE PLEASURES OF DEEP READING

Researching a non-fiction book is like diving to the bottom of the ocean and looking for treasure. You often don't know what you're going to find or even where to look.

Some days, you'll return to the surface with valuable pearls. Other days, you'll come back with nothing more than yellow plastic bottles, rusty cans and a chewed-up plastic Barbie doll to show for your trouble.

You can increase your chances of bringing back treasure through deep, active reading.

If you're reading a paperback or hardback book, annotate it with a pen or write in the margins. Affix Post-it notes or jot down your thoughts on index cards.

If you're reading a digital book, on a Kindle for example, highlight key sentences. Whatever your medium of choice, look for:

- Key statistics
- Interesting findings and insights
- Sentences that sum up the book's controlling idea
- Common concepts running throughout the book
- Sections you agree/disagree with
- Compelling turns of phrase
- Unique stories and insights

Once you finish reading a book, go back and review your notes, annotations and so on. If you're using a Kindle or e-reader, export your notes to your computer.

I also like looking on sites like Goodreads to see what other readers thought about the book. I enjoy reviewing their highlighted quotes, key takeaways and more.

Once you're finished reading and marking up a book, get ready to arrange your research.

MIND MAPPING YOUR RESEARCH

Mind mapping is a great way of arranging your research (and even your book; see next chapter) into different topics. This creative technique will help you connect different ideas and offers a means of reviewing a topic without having to re-read a book later.

It shouldn't take more than ten or 15 minutes to mind map a topic or even a book you've read. You'll need:

- A blank piece of paper (A4 size or larger)
- Some multi-coloured pens or markers
- Your book notes, highlights and annotations

Now, turn the paper on its side and write down your topic in the centre of your mind map. While reviewing your notes, draw out each of the connecting ideas using different colour pens. Thicken your branches at the root and thin them out as they move away from the central idea.

Using red, blue, black and green pens or markers will help you create a more memorable mind map. Sketch images representing concepts you came across while reading, and reorder your branches or draw another mind map if you need to.

You should be able to see the central idea and the overall structure of a book, as well as how different concepts relate to each other.

You don't have to become a Picasso of mind maps or obsess about the structure either. They're for you and you alone.

THE ART OF WRITING A NON-FICTION BOOK

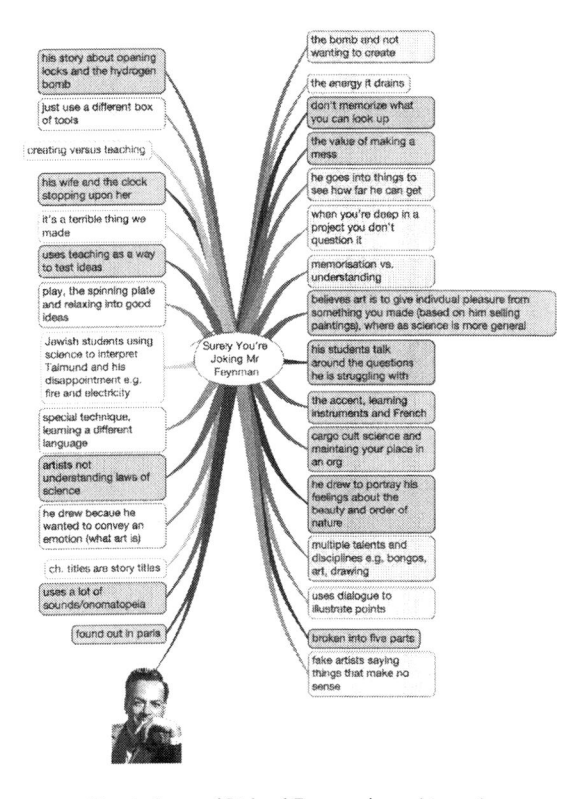

My mind map of Richard Feynman's autobiography

HOW TO TEACH YOUR READERS ABOUT A CONCEPT (LIKE RICHARD FEYNMAN)

One time while working as a journalist, I had to write a feature article about the best computer keyboards. I spent seven hours reading reviews on Amazon and watching videos on YouTube.

Was I doing the work?

God, no.

The article was about keyboards, not the atom bomb. You can only spend so much time reading before it turns into procrastination. So start using your research as part of your writing.

Do it sometime before they excavate your remains from beneath a stack of books, index cards and half-drunk cups of coffee.

As for the how?

Feynman offers four steps for understanding and teaching complicated topics.

Step One: Choose Your Concept or Topic

Think back to the work you completed earlier. You've picked a controlling idea for your non-fiction book, and each one of your chapters should have a central topic.

Now, read up on each of these topics. Arrange your research and take care to put into practice (or least interrogate) as much as you can. Do this before you start writing.

Later, you'll be able to tell stories about what you did and what happened next.

If you offer your perspective, you'll avoid the problems Feynman's Brazilian students faced. Your book will become more than regurgitated information.

Step Two: Teach Your Topic

Did you ever think, *But, I need to carry out more research.*

Well, when you're up to your eyeballs in mind maps, dog-eared books and tattered index cards, it's time to open up the blank page and get going.

Write down what you know, what you did, what you experienced and what your readers should do.

Use simple language that a small child would understand. This will force you to take apart complicated concepts and put them back together for your readers.

Be concrete. Provide practical examples. Give your readers exercises and takeaways they can use immediately.

For example, while I was training to run a marathon, I read a popular training book, full of day-by-day training plans for athletes of all levels. Suffice to say, this book sold a lot of copies.

Step Three: Go Back And Fill In Gaps in Your Knowledge

Non-fiction writing often feels like painting. You'll spend time going back over your work. Softening an introduction. Adding colour to a conclusion. Touching up a chapter here. Smoothing out a chapter there, and so on – until your chapter and your book achieves a distinctive look.

As you write about concepts in your book, you will naturally come across gaps in your knowledge. For example, you may need to look up someone's date of birth. Or you may need to go back to your research and pull out another idea to strengthen your arguments.

When this happens, *don't stop*. Mark up your manuscript or highlight the section and keep going.

During your rewrites, fill in the gaps in your book (and by extension, your knowledge about the topic).

Step Four: Review and Simplify Your Work

One of Feynman's famous principles about science is that you "must not fool yourself – and you are the easiest person to fool." This principle applies to non-fiction book writing too.

Don't presume you understand a topic if you've relied on complicated language, jargon and the original author's turns of phrase.

Despite what some authors think, you're not doing your job if you bamboozle your readers with technical concepts and lots of facts. Challenge yourself to refine your work until it's as clear as possible. During each rewrite, ask questions like:

- Do I understand what I'm writing about?
- Have I made assumptions about myself or my readers?
- Have I said this in the easiest way possible for my readers?
- Have I explained technical terms, jargon and so on?
- What can I take out?
- *What else* can I take out?
- Is this clear?
- Is this concise?

- Would Richard Feynman approve?

Surely You're Reading, Mr. Feynman!

Don't be afraid by the name(s) on the front of a book or if you're reading something by an 'expert'. Once you get deep into research and have shattered the ice protecting a topic, you'll find many conflicting – and even lousy – ideas.

Several years after his Brazilian escapade, the US Board of Education asked Feynman to serve on a curriculum commission. They wanted him to choose textbooks for the state of California.

Against his better judgment, Feynman agreed, and he looked over the proposed schoolbooks based on the merits of their advice.

He set up a special shelf in his study downstairs and stacked the books 17 feet high, and he began to read through them. Feynman said his wife likened the experience to living over a volcano.

He described her experience living with him, saying:

> It would be quiet for a while, but then all of a sudden, 'BLLLLLOOOOOOWWWWW!!!!'–there would be a big explosion from the 'volcano' below.

Feynman blew up loudly and frequently.

Many of the textbooks were lousy, false and hurried. He didn't like the examples within them and couldn't see how they would help elementary students learn scientific topics.

Feynman became increasingly frustrated with the "useless, mixed-up, ambiguous and confusing books." He complained:

> Everything was written by somebody who didn't know what the hell they were talking about, so it was a little bit wrong, always!

While on the commission, Feynman read a math book that 65 engineers approved. Feynman knew there were some good engineers at the company. But he argued taking the opinions of 65 engineers to write a book will produce an average one at best:

It was once again the problem of averaging the length of the emperor's nose... It would have been far better to have the company decide who their better engineers were and to have them look at the book.

When Feynman found out other people on the commission didn't even read the books, he resigned and wrote the experience off as wasted effort.

If you want to avoid producing an average book, or one no-one reads, don't water down your opinions. Avoid writing for the masses or deferring to 'so-called experts'.

Be honest about your opinions. Have the courage of your convictions. Hold your research and topic to account.

THE CURRENTS OF GREAT RESEARCH

Theoretical physicist. Nobel Prize winner. Renowned bongo player.

Richard Feynman had a lot of credits to his name. He was also the kind of reader and non-fiction writer who could tell the difference between a good book and a lousy book. Between memorising an idea and understanding it. Between interrogating a concept and regurgitating it.

He understood it's not enough to know an idea. You must understand the thinking behind it...and this is particularly true if you're going to write about it.

The best non-fiction books contain more than the author's experiences. A current of research flows beneath each chapter, giving the book a life of its own.

Like Feynman, it's your job as an author to break through the frozen ice protecting many books and research sources. Figure out what you agree or disagree with and how concepts and ideas relate to each other.

Commit to reading books, to understanding the thinking behind them and to putting into practice what you find. Just remember to point readers to your sources at the back of *your book*.

If you master the research process, you'll be able to connect abstract ideas to your experiences and your readers' problems.

They'll thank you for it.

YOUR WRITING EXERCISES

- Consider the last book that you read: What were the key topics within this book? How do these topics relate to each other, and can you connect them to ideas in other books?
- Create a simple mind map of the last book you read, reflecting on the key takeaways. Now, practice doing this for each book you read and store these mind maps together, so you can review your research.

CRACKING THE BOOK OUTLINING CODE

"Give me six hours to chop down a tree, and I will spend the first four sharpening the axe." – Abraham Lincoln

So you've interviewed your ideal readers, filled your swipe file and you know what your non-fiction book must deliver... now what?

Well like a grandmaster surveying the chessboard and planning their end-game, you need to be able to step back from your ideas.

You don't want to discover thirty or forty hours into your book that you're up to your eyeballs in research and writing about the wrong things.

Professional non-fiction writers know how to arrange their thoughts... and they often rely on outlines before they put ink on the blank page.

You could write from the seat of your pants, but this uncertain way of writing lends itself better to fiction or literary writing.

A book outline will help you see if you're true to your book's controlling idea, if your arguments stand up and if you're writing what your readers want.

CALCULATING YOUR TARGET WORD COUNT

Your book's ideal word count depends on your sub-genre. Writing books, like this, are typically short while historical biographies often run over 100,000 words.

That said, many successful non-fiction books are approximately 50,000-80,000 words.

For example:

- Malcolm Gladwell's *Blink* is over 70,000 words.
- James Altucher's *Choose Yourself* is 74,500 words.
- Michael Hyatt's *Living Forward* is 64,480 words.
- Seth Godin's *New York Times* best-seller *The Dip* is approximately 24,000 words.

If you're unsure about an appropriate target, buy five of the most popular books in your niche and estimate their word counts.

UNDERSTANDING THE STRUCTURE OF A SUCCESSFUL BOOK

Act one and act three typically comprise 60% of your word count, while act two comprises 40% (excluding your introduction, references and so on).

Stray too far from this rule of thumb, and you risk unbalancing your book.

It's a classic form of storytelling with a distinct beginning, middle and end. The first act connects to the second and the second to the third, forming an arc that satisfies readers.

Act one is the beginning of your book.

Usually, act one begins with a memorable scene, a dramatic incident or a call-to-action. In this act, hook your reader by introducing a problem or by setting up the story driving your book.

Act two is the middle build of your book.

In the meat of your book, elaborate on the problem and heighten the conflict. Show what's at stake and present challenges you or the reader must overcome.

Act three, the final third, brings resolution or closure for your readers.

It includes a climax where you either solve the big problem your book is addressing or offer a resolution. The reader experiences a payoff or gets the solution they paid for.

In the case of this book, the first act reveals what happens when you decide you want to become a non-fiction author (the hook).

The second act covers gaining the skills and work habits of a professional author (the build).

The third act addresses finishing your work and embracing the freedom that comes with being a published author (the payoff).

Obviously, there are exceptions to the three-act structure, such as collections of essays, literary journalism and so on.

That said, the three-act structure is a universal concept. Most aspiring non-fiction authors should embrace it as it will bring a sense of balance to your book.

Now, let's pick an approach for creating your three-act structure.

THE ANALOGUE APPROACH: USING INDEX CARDS

I spent a year reading books about creativity as part of my research for *The Power of Creativity*. I scribbled in the margins of these books, journaled about what I found and bored anyone who asked me, "Where do great ideas come from?"

Then I spent four months organising my ideas. I free wrote about creativity. I extracted ideas, and I turned them into provisional chapter titles. And I recorded these on sixty index cards.

On each card, I created a rough list of ideas in the form of five to ten bullet points. I noted other books and stories to reference. Then, I pinned these index cards to a wall near where I write so that I could live with this outline.

I spent a month working on this outline before transferring it to my computer and expanding on each bullet point.

Did I plan my book like this because I'm an obsessive weirdo? Perhaps.

But I wanted to spend as much mental energy as possible during the planning stage. When the time came to write, I felt more confident about the direction of my book.

Outlining my book with pen and paper, and then later with Evernote, helped me figure out what I wanted to write about in each chapter. It also helped me identify gaps in my research and problems in my work UPFRONT.

Obviously, my outline and table of contents evolved. But, when I was starting from 'Total word count: 0', my outline served as a map. It saved me time and helped me beat procrastination.

Step 1: Categorise Your Book's Key Ideas

You'll need a red and blue pen, a packet of 3x5-inch index cards and a table where you can arrange your ideas. Now, write down a single idea or concept in red pen, one per index card.

Each idea should correspond to the central concept behind a book chapter. For example, in the case of this chapter, I wrote down 'Arranging Your Ideas' at the top of an index card.

Step 2: Expand on Your Key Ideas

Write down five to ten bullet points with your blue pen. Your points should be clear, short and snappy. Try to sum up the key parts forming your single idea. Use sub-bullet points if necessary. If you make a mistake, cross out your ideas or tear up a card and start again.

Step 3: Flesh out Your Entire Book

Keep going until you have broken down all the big ideas for your book on index cards.

Don't get caught up in the exact wording. Your job is to get the essence of each idea out of your head or swipe file and onto the index cards.

The larger your book, the more index cards you'll need. You can outline an article using just three or four index cards, whereas you may need as many as 50-60 cards for a non-fiction book.

Step 4: Arrange Your Ideas (and the Structure of Your Book)

Lay your index cards beside each other on a table. Rearrange your cards, taking care to remove irrelevant ideas and add new ones. Do this until you're happy with the structure of your book and the key topics in each chapter.

Typically, I sort each index card by putting the cards for:

- Act one on the left of the table
- Act two in the centre
- Act three on the far right

Then, I create another section for cards I feel unsure about.

Step 5: Live with Your Book Structure

Spend at least a week considering what's on your index cards and the structure of your book.

I like using a whiteboard for this process. It's less intrusive than taking over a table for days or weeks. Plus, I don't have to worry about the kids or my dog knocking my whiteboard (and my book) over.

Step 6: Start Writing Your Book

You don't need to nail the structure of your book before you start filling the blank page. You can always go back and reframe this structure as you write. But doing this work up front will reduce the amount of time you spend (and the hair you pull out) on a painful rewrite.

If you follow this process of refining, adding and subtracting, you stand a better chance of writing a book true to your controlling idea and what readers want.

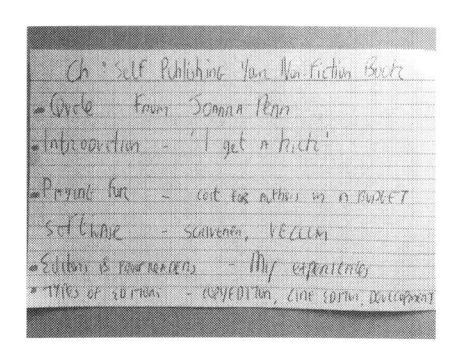

One of my index cards that outlines a chapter in this book

HOW TO KNOW IF THIS APPROACH IS FOR YOU

Pen and paper and other analogue tools come with fewer distractions than a computer. The smell of ink, the dry feel of paper, and a stack of well-worn books are more tangible than any click, buzz or notification from a writing application.

This approach is for you if sometimes wish you could plunge your hand into the screen and get a physical feel for your book.

THE DIGITAL APPROACH: USING SPREADSHEETS

When I was a pale-faced writer with more hair, I told anyone who would listen, "I hate spreadsheets. They're for right-side-of-the-brain thinkers, and they're for accountants who spend too much time looking at profit and loss statements."

Ah, how wrong I was.

You can break down an intimidating non-fiction book using a spreadsheet and write it faster. Zooming out to arrange your ideas is faster than playing with blocks of text in a word processor.

Remember, you're not going to write in the spreadsheet. Instead, your goal is to create a system for categorising and organising ideas for your book.

You can open up on the blank page later.

Step 1: Set up Your Spreadsheet

Create a spreadsheet, and name it after a potential title for your book. Label column A in the spreadsheet as 'Act', column B as 'Chapter', column C as 'Idea' and column D as 'Word count'.

Step 2: Pick an Idea for a Chapter in Your Book

In column B of the spreadsheet, write down the central idea underpinning a chapter you're going to write. Don't worry if you're unclear on what each chapter is about. You can always revise for clarity (and fill in the details of column B) later.

Step 3: Break Down Your Idea for This Chapter

Review your notes, research and reader interview transcript. Then in column C, write down your ideas for the key sections in this chapter. A sentence or two describing each idea should suffice, and you should aim for five to six ideas.

In my case, the key sections include 'Finding out What Readers Want', 'Mastering Your Tools', 'Acting on Feedback' and so on.

Step 4: Set Word Counts for Each Section in Your Book

In column D, write down your target word count for each section. Ideally, each section is the same length, give or take 10%.

You don't want to write an 800-word introduction for a 1,500-word book chapter, just as you don't want a book with a 40,000-word hook and a 2,000-word payoff.

Seek out balance between each chapter and section in your book.

Step 5: Complete Your Spreadsheet

Now, while reviewing your notes, interview transcripts and research, work from right to left in your spreadsheet.

Write down the key:

- Sections in each chapter
- Chapters in your book
- Acts in your book

It should take you about 15-20 minutes to arrange ideas for a single chapter and several hours to arrange each chapter into an act.

Step 6: Review Your Ideas

Now, review your ideas, moving and re-categorising them as required. Again, this will take several hours to get right. Use copy-and-paste to speed things up and re-categorise your ideas by section, chapter and act.

Step 7: Start Writing

Now, you should have a working outline that serves as your North Star. You've broken your large and intimidating writing project into small, digestible pieces. You can tackle these each day.

You see, it's much easier to show up and write a 300-word section for Chapter Four than it is to sit down with the intention of 'working on my book'.

Act	Chapter title	Points to cover	Target Word Count
1	So You Want to Write Your First Book?	Decide What Type of Writer You Are Establish what your book is about Robert McKee Ideas and concepts within a book What aspiring writers vs actually authors do i.e. bar analogy	2200
1	Cracking the book outlining code	Plotter or pantser Provide guidelines for both approaches	2200
1	Finding Out What Your Readers Expect (And Who They Are)	Interview them Research forums etc. Marketing vs writing Coming up with a controlling idea and positioning statements Provide templates and examples	2200
2	Researching Your Book. The Noble Prize Approach	Types of research The story of Richard Feynman teaching and in Brazil Step 1-4 Importance of reading	2200
2	Taking Charge Your Tools Before They Take Charge of You	Owning your tools Tools I use Analogue vs digital How to dictate a book chapter	2200
2	Taming That Unruly First Draft	Get it out of your head I still can't get started Why you should write every day Knowing when your first draft is done Don't start on page 1	2200
3	Mastering Your Writing Self Like a Zen Master	Setting up your place where you write The tools I use: Scrivener, Google Drive etc. What you can ignore Tools as a form of procrastination Lack of self-belief and turning it into fuel	2200
3	Self-editing Your Book Like a Smart Author Should	Work with an editor How to find an editor Marking up your manuscript Round 1: Editing the Structure of Your Book Chapter Round 2: Editing Your Book Chapter in Relation to Other Book Chapters Round 3: Line-editing Your Book Chapter Proofing and Fact-checking Your Work Provide tips e.g. using the active voice	2200
3	Finishing (And Shipping) Your Work	Set a date What to do when you finish Money, freedom, success. Deciding what to write next	2200

What a book outline in a spreadsheet looks like

HOW TO KNOW IF THIS APPROACH IS FOR YOU

This approach is great for writers who are comfortable with digital tools and don't get distracted. It's faster than using index cards because you can manipulate the structure of your book on-screen.

A spreadsheet outline of your book offers a bird's-eye view that can help you fix problems upfront. For example, you can check word counts for each section and then address any imbalances.

But I Still Hate Spreadsheets!

If you're struggling to get to grips with a spreadsheet, create a mind map of your book and of each of the chapters within your book using a tool like iMindMap.

In the previous chapter, I explain how to use mind maps for your research, and you can follow the same process for your writing.

THE PLEASURE OF ARRANGING YOUR IDEAS

Most professional writers base their books on meticulous research and lots of caffeine.

Once a week, devote yourself to reading your notes, journal entries, research and so on, taking care to categorise what you find.

Consider:

- Which ideas are the strongest, and how can I build on them?
- Which ideas are the weakest, and can I remove them?
- What ideas am I missing?
- How can I reorder my ideas and clarify my writing?
- What are the obvious gaps in my research?

When you review your ideas, you can fix your book's structure without line-editing sentences, paragraphs and sections.

What's more, it's always a delight to find a useful idea in your notes that you'd forgotten.

Pick an approach for outlining your book and work on your structure until it feels solid. You don't need to arrange every little idea before you start writing.

By all means, set yourself a hard deadline if you're worried about overplanning your book.

Once you've established a three-act structure, you'll have a strong foundation for your book, and that's what we're going to build on next.

YOUR WRITING EXERCISES

- Calculate the target word count of your book (and each act) based on other popular books within your sub-genre.
- Front-load the hard work of writing a non-fiction book by organising your ideas using either index cards or a spreadsheet.

TAMING THAT UNRULY FIRST DRAFT

"I have no money, no resources, no hopes. I am the happiest man alive." – Henry Miller

I once wrote the first draft of a book chapter that smelt so bad, I had to open up the office window while reading it.

It's a good thing my first drafts are for me alone, and yours should be too. When you sit down to write a first draft, you may lack confidence or feel uninspired by what you're about to do.

Today, it's you alone wrestling with your ideas and stories, and if you pin one to the page only to decide you don't like the look of it, nobody needs to know.

Most writers, even successful ones, don't write good first drafts. They're more concerned with getting the words out of their heads and onto the blank page.

They know they can fix their drafts during a rewrite.

You may feel like you're writing with a crayon in your mouth, and that's okay.

Most successful authors don't experience moments of white-hot inspiration while writing their first draft.

Instead, there's a determined soul plugging away at their manuscript, one sentence at a time. He or she looks at their word count or the clock and all the while thinking, "It'll do for now. I'm almost there. I can fix this later."

WORK ON YOUR FIRST DRAFT EVERY DAY… UNTIL IT'S DONE

The American non-fiction writer Henry Miller (1891-1980) produced dozens of books, essays and pamphlets during his career. He often wrote about his personal experiences in vivid and shocking detail, and many of his books were banned.

Like many aspiring writers, Miller had little money during the early part of his career. He spent ten years writing in obscurity in Paris relying on the support of fellow writer (and lover) Anaïs Nin.

Miller approached his first drafts as if they were a voyage of discovery, and first drafts often terrified him.

He said:

> I began in absolute chaos and darkness, in a bog or swamp of ideas and emotions and experiences. Even now I do not consider myself a writer, in the ordinary sense of the word. I am a man telling the story of his life, a process which appears more and more inexhaustible as I go on.

Successful authors like Miller sit down in front of the blank page almost every day. They don't wait until the weekend, for inspiration to strike or to feel confident about writing a draft.

They do the work because writing is their job and not a hobby. They write more lousy first drafts than amateurs… and they discover what does and doesn't work.

The author and blogger James Altucher is a more contemporary example. He specialises in non-fiction, and he writes one article a day, every day.

He says:

You can't be a master in one day. You have to improve a little every day.

Now, I'm no Henry Miller, but here's the creative workflow I use to fumble through the darkness and work on an intimidating first draft.

- I go to a quiet room, office, library or coffee shop.
- Depending on where I am, I brew or order a cup of coffee.
- I disconnect my computer from the internet.
- I put my phone in airplane mode.
- I open up Scrivener.
- I arrange the outline for the chapter in question.
- I set a timer for 30 minutes.
- I write, keep my fingers moving and avoid stopping to edit myself (This is harder than it sounds).
- When the buzzer sounds, I stand up and take a two-minute break.
- After this break, I review my outline and notes.
- I repeat my 30 minute writing session two to four times until I hit the day's word count.

When you turn up in front of the blank page to write a first draft, forget your past accomplishments and failures. You may have written a hundred, a thousand or even ten thousand words yesterday. Or maybe you didn't write at all.

Today, you just have to write a lousy first draft... because there are no *good* first drafts. The only job of a first draft is to exist.

You can fix those messy mistakes, take out what doesn't work and put in what's needed during the second, third and fourth drafts.

WHY YOU SHOULDN'T START WRITING YOUR FIRST DRAFT ON PAGE ONE

Many professional writers appear to possess superpowers (Miller, I'm looking at you).

When they sit down to write, they stack up chapter after chapter. They smash through daily word counts that we mere mortals can only dream of.

So does a radioactive spider bite these writers while they were thumbing through the dusty final pages of *Tropic of Cancer*?

Well, if you press a professional writer long enough, they'll tell you that writing the beginning of a first draft is the hardest part.

An introduction to a non-fiction book, or even a chapter, explains or sets up what's about to happen.

But how can you write an introduction if you don't know what comes next?

A conclusion wraps up what was just said. Again, how can you write one if you don't know what you just said!

Whether you're a plotter or a pantser, it's a perplexing conundrum that feels ripped straight from *The Matrix*.

Most professional writers don't care much for conundrums, not when they have a deadline, kids to feed and an overweight cat to manicure.

Instead, they lay out their notes and outlines (if they have them), and they look for an easy way into their first drafts. Then, they often start in the middle of their books and write forwards...or backwards.

Opening up in the middle of your book will help you gain momentum faster. You could:

- Start writing from chapter five or 25, or from anywhere that inspires you.
- Start writing by saying something like, "Then, there I/he/she was..."
- Begin in the middle of a sentence, paragraph or idea.

- Write as close to the end as you can get without stumping yourself.
- Write about what you think of some research or findings for your book.
- Write up an interview you completed for your book.
- Write about a problem you or your readers are having that relates to your book.

Using this approach, write to the beginning, write to the end or jump around if you have to. Work through your first draft paragraph by paragraph, page by page and cup of coffee by cup of coffee.

I STILL CAN'T GET STARTED!

Have you ever looked at the blank page and found it difficult to get started? Well, it was Ernest Hemingway who said:

> There is nothing to writing. All you do is sit down at a typewriter and bleed.

It's no wonder many new writers struggle when they start sitting down in front of the blank page regularly.

So lower the bar.

Pick a single idea from your book and see where it takes you. Give yourself permission to write nonsense for ten, twenty or even sixty minutes. Write for the sheer hell of it without fear or expectation.

When a runner is training for a big race, he or she practices by competing in shorter or more low-key races before the main event. These training races are more about building self-confidence than performing.

When you're starting off, it's enough to turn up in front of the blank page and limber up too. Later on, once you're writing at pace, you can rewrite your earlier drafts or even discard them for something better.

You should also set yourself up for success each day. Prolific writers know how important it is to start writing quickly. So they go easy on themselves.

Ernest Hemingway famously stopped writing in the middle of a sentence so he'd know exactly where to resume the following day.

Here's what happens when you stop writing before you empty the tank:

Your subconscious brain continues working while you're sleeping, working or showering.

Then, when you sit down to write the following day, you'll find it much easier to pick up from where you left off.

WHAT TO EXPECT FROM YOUR FIRST DRAFT

Many writers call their first pass 'the vomit draft'.

In an interview with Tim Ferris, American non-fiction author Neil Strauss said:

> …your first draft is only for you. No one is ever going to see it, so you don't have to worry about it. You're not going to turn it in. You're not going to show it to friends to evaluate – because it's only for you.

So don't stop to edit yourself, straighten up your sentences or to see if what you wrote sounds reasonable.

If you begin fixing your draft, you'll engage a different part of your brain, the part that belongs to your internal editor. Your editor has a place in the writing process but not when you're trying to reach a target word count.

He or she wants to censor your work and doesn't care that you're trying to hit a word count by the end of your writing session.

So expect misplaced apostrophes. Become friends with dangling modifiers. Invite those hackneyed ideas to dinner.

Don't feel surprised when typos slip out and when your hooks are so clichéd that they make *Days of Our Lives* looks like *Hamlet*.

Your first draft is for getting creative ideas and research onto the page. It takes many revisions to turn a first draft into a book you can publish, and you're going to do all that when you invite your internal editor out to play later on.

HOW LONG IS A GOOD FIRST DRAFT?

First drafts are as long as they need to be. The ideal length also depends on the conventions of your sub-genre.

By now, you should understand your genre's average word count, and you can use this as a target.

So:

- If you write 1,000 words of your first draft a day, you'll produce 6,000 words a week and still be able to take Sunday off.
- If you write 6,000 words a week, you'll have a draft finished somewhere between four and 12 weeks, depending on the length and sub-genre of your book.
- If you write 6,000 words a week for a year, you'll produce over 300,000 words, which is far longer than most popular non-fiction books.

Okay, you won't be able to use a lot of your 300,000 words... but there's gold in there. You'll find it when you sift through your words, ideas and stories during the editing process.

Remember, your goal is to finish writing your first draft so that you have something to rewrite and edit.

While working on the second or third draft, you can gather more people around your writing and fix your messy mistakes. Enlist unsuspecting family members, friends, an editor and even first readers.

Ask what they found confusing in your draft, what worked and what bored them. Then, go about fixing these problems during your next rewrite.

A NOTE ON LOGISTICS

A first draft will cover your desk, floors and even your walls. You've got to crack open a part of yourself and spill what's inside onto the page. You can't do this if you're working in chaos or you don't know where anything is.

When the American poet Raymond Carver was starting off, he wrote on notepads in his car.

The American novelist John Cheever wrote most of his best works alone in a basement in New York wearing just a pair of boxers.

The British author Virginia Woolf worked in a small writing room in her garden, constructed from a wooden toolshed beneath a loft.

These authors, like most true professionals, went to the same place regularly to work on their first drafts.

While writing a book, I often cover my desk (and the ground) with index cards, books, torn-up first drafts and wrappers from half-eaten chocolate bars.

So you're going to need a place to write... and to make a mess each day, without interruption. Creativity demands lots of space, but by all means, tidy up when you're done.

KNOWING WHEN YOU'RE FINISHED WITH A FIRST DRAFT

Raymond Carver spent weeks, months or even years working on his poetry, essays and short stories. And yet, even he recognised the value of writing his first drafts quickly. He said:

> It doesn't take that long to do the first draft of the story, that usually happens in one sitting, but it does take a while to do the various versions of the story. I've done as many as twenty or thirty drafts of a story.

So don't overburden your first draft with expectations. That can come later when you rewrite and edit your book. Once you've finished the first draft of your book, you can take the crayon out of your mouth and relax.

Now, you have a body of writing that you can mould and shape into something your readers will enjoy.

YOUR WRITING EXERCISES

- Set a target word count for your book, and then break it down into targets for each chapter. Now, pick these off one-by-one.
- Do whatever it takes to get the words out of your head and onto the blank page. Record a first draft into the voice app on your phone. Dictate it. Sell your firstborn if you must.

MASTERING YOUR WRITING SELF LIKE A ZEN MASTER

"*From a certain point onward there is no longer any turning back. That is the point that must be reached.*" – Franz Kafka

You're excited about the progress of your book, but half-way through, you stop and wonder...

Will people really care about what I've got to say? How will this pay my bills anyway? What if I'm wasting my time?

These negative thoughts fester in your mind, and your lack of self-belief paralyses you.

So you stop working on your ideas. You decide against finishing your first or second draft. You put off editing what you've written. You leave your book in a drawer and don't look at it for weeks or months at a time.

Fear not: many authors before you have faced (and overcome) this problem.

EVEN FRANZ KAFKA LACKED SELF-BELIEF

Born in 1883 in Prague, Franz Kafka worked a demanding job as a lawyer for the Worker's Accident Insurance. Each day, he worked from 8 or 9 a.m. until 2 or 3 p.m.

Then, he ate lunch and took a long nap. Sometime around 11 p.m., after dinner and exercise, Kafka wrote until he fell asleep.

Kafka famously said about what it takes to fill the blank page:

> You need not leave your room. Remain sitting at your table and listen. You need not even listen, simply wait, just learn to become quiet, and still, and solitary. The world will freely offer itself to you to be unmasked. It has no choice; it will roll in ecstasy at your feet.

Throughout his life, Kafka suffered from boils, depression and anxiety while not writing. He was an indecisive insomniac who was afraid of living and terrified by the prospects of his death.

He was painfully aware of the toll day-to-day life and ill-health took from his creative work and what he had to do to overcome his problems.

While living in Prague, he published *The Metamorphosis*, (a chilling novella of a man who turns into an insect) to no great acclaim. He also wrote several other books and stories, but he didn't believe in their merits. After all, this was a man who said:

> Writing is utter solitude, the descent into the cold abyss of oneself.

After contracting tuberculosis, Kafka quit his job to recuperate. He continued to struggle with poor health, and fearing that he wouldn't live long, he told his friend Max Brod to destroy his writings once he died.

Despite these personal and physical problems, Kafka wrote consistently. He kept his strict daily routine and cultivated tremendous self-discipline.

Towards the end of his life, he travelled to Vienna for treatment at a sanatorium before dying in Kierling in Austria in 1924.

After his death, Brod read through Kafka's papers and decided to ignore his old friend's request. Brod believed in his friend's writing... even if Kafka didn't.

The following year, Brod published *The Trial*. It's a short, dark novel about a man locked in a hopeless court system.

Afterwards, Brod published *The Castle*. This novel is about a protagonist fighting against the authorities ruling over a village. Over the following years, Kafka's writing became popular in Eastern communist Europe.

Today, we recognise Kafka as one of the literary heavyweights of the 19th century, and yet he never believed in himself.

So you see, it's normal to lack self-belief; the trick is to handle it so that you can learn how to gain confidence as a writer.

STOP WITH THE COMPARISONITIS

It's not polite to talk about jealousy but...

As much as I love writers like Kafka, I cower in the shadows of their natural talents, beneath the towering ambition of the works.

I sometimes compare their accomplishments to my own, and I reach a standstill with my writing.

Even when I think of more contemporary writers, their popularity is enough for me to question what I'm attempting.

No new writer in their natural mind should compare themselves to the likes of famous authors like Malcolm Gladwell, Truman Capote or even Kafka.

And yet, it's difficult.

Their creative works wait for us in bookstores, at airports, on television, all over the internet, on Twitter, Facebook and more.

When I hear a voice whispering, "Look how great Gladwell is, and then there's you, writing about the wrong things," or, "Truman Capote never blogged, why are you wasting your time?" I want to quit.

I have to remind myself what I'm looking at is the summit of their public successes and not their private failures. Their successes represent what they reveal to the world. But nobody sees the abandoned manuscripts, the torn-up pages and unfinished books.

Know that when you compare yourself to successful writers, all you see is what you lack and not how far you've come.

This brings me to...

USE YOUR LACK OF SELF-BELIEF AS FUEL

If you only write about your successes and how well things are going, your readers won't be able to stomach this sanitised version of your ideas.

They want to hear the grubby details.

Several years ago, I became a father for the first time. It was a happy time, but after my son was born, I dreamt about death and how my life would end.

Late at night, when everyone was asleep, I lay in bed clenching and unclenching my fists and trying not to worry, a little like Kafka.

I knew I wasn't depressed, but I worried there was something wrong with me. Then a friend (also a recent father) confessed having the same thoughts.

I learnt as we get older, it's natural to consider mortality and death. To pretend death doesn't exist is to live in ignorance of the bond we all share. So I used these insights to write an essay about becoming a father for the first time and what this meant for me.

So the next time something goes wrong, when you fail and wonder if you've still got it, pause.

Consider what went wrong or what you're struggling with, and ask yourself, *How can I turn this private failure into fuel for my writing?*

Look...

Kafka suffered from anxiety, depression and ill-health throughout his life. And yet, he drew on these experiences for his writing.

In *The Metamorphosis*, his protagonist Gregor Samsa says:

I cannot make you understand. I cannot make anyone understand what is happening inside me. I cannot even explain it to myself.

That's an insight that could have only come from Kafka's inner struggles. So, when writing your book, bleed into it. Because it's all material.

Because it all counts.

PUT ON YOUR LIFE JACKET

When you doubt yourself, it's natural to want to postpone writing because you're tired, bored or 'just not feeling it.' But it's your job to swim through these choppy waters and continue your journey towards becoming an author.

It's not always easy, which is why most successful authors keep to a strict schedule. Like a doctor or an engineer, they rise early, work late or go to the same place every day to work.

Like Kafka, they write because they have to and not just when they feel the hand of inspiration on their shoulders.

Remember, every writer is at a different stage along their journey. For you, it could be something as simple as writing 500 words a day for 31 days. It could be finishing your first chapter. Or it could be self-publishing your first book.

Recognise these small markers as you sail past them.

It's up to you to strap on a life jacket when the stormy waters of self-doubt threaten to pull you under, because committing to your book means developing the mental strength to silence negative inner-monologue… and keep writing.

USING A WRITING LOG

When I'm writing a book, I use a timer on my computer to track my hours and a spreadsheet to record the status of each chapter. I also use Google Calendar to manage my deadlines and a To-Do list for my commitments.

At the end of a writing session, I record how long I spent writing, what I wrote and my word count or writing milestone. At the end of the week, I total up each column.

Sometimes, I try to beat this total the following week. Knowing what I accomplished (or failed at) helps me see if I'm progressing or lying to myself.

I'm a little weird when it comes to tracking my time, but I blame Ernest Hemingway. He wrote standing up and kept a large board next to where he worked. It was there, he tracked his daily word count so as "not to kid myself."

If you want to master yourself, keep a writing log of your progress. Review the past month, three months, the past year and even the past four years.

Don't over think it. It should only take a few minutes each day to record your progress. You could track:

- Your daily word count
- Your target word count for the week or month
- How long you spent writing
- What you wrote
- What you're going to write next
- The current status of each chapter in your book

Do you need help tracking your writing? If so, I've created a free writing log that will help you manage the progress of your book.

It's part of your book writing bonus that you can get at becomeawritertoday.com/author

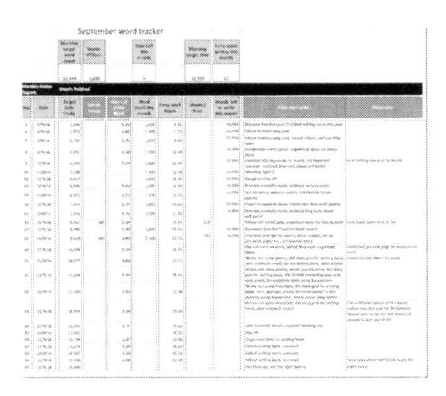

An example of a busy month from my writing log

GAINING CONFIDENCE IN YOURSELF

Kafka's writings only found a rightful audience after he died. Now, I wouldn't like for you to wait that long before you publish your book, start earning money from your writing and find success.

I spent a lot of time waiting to publish my articles and books and for editors and readers to find me.

I waited too long.

So, several years ago, I committed to publishing one blog post a week (perfection, be damned!) and to sending it to readers and subscribers of my email list.

These days, I try to do this every Thursday. I can only do this by keeping to a strict writing schedule, writing even when I don't feel like it and tracking my progress. Some weeks, when Thursday morning comes around, I imagine reasons not to press publish, not to press send.

'You're wasting your time, Bryan. Nobody will read this. Your ideas are half-baked, and you've told all the wrong stories.'

It doesn't help that writing often means getting comfortable with failure.

And yet...

When I press publish, when I press send, it's a minor victory.

So here's the thing:

Self-belief is something writers of all levels struggle with during their careers. All you have to do is learn from your mistakes (because they will happen) and how to gain confidence as a writer.

Today, you can get feedback about your work easily and share your writing and ideas with the world. You don't need a patron like Max Brod or a wealth of resources to do this either.

You can email versions of your book to trusted friends or colleagues. You can blog. You can hire an editor. You can self-publish.

Once you get your ideas out into the world, you'll see you already have everything you need to master yourself and your writing.

All you have to do is to be brave enough to recognise your lack of self-belief for what it is. A marker on your journey towards becoming an accomplished non-fiction author.

YOUR WRITING EXERCISES

- Consider a personal or professional failure related to your book topic and write about it.
- Keep a writing log. There, record your daily progress, and use these insights to improve your craft.

SELF-EDITING YOUR BOOK UNTIL IT'S GOOD ENOUGH TO PUBLISH

―

"Grammar is a piano I play by ear." – Joan Didion

Learning how to self-edit a book is a little liking having sex for the first time. At first, you may not understand what you're doing or where anything goes, but with practice, it gets better.

Before you even pick up a red pen, finish writing your book's first draft. Otherwise, you risk turning into the frustrated aspiring author who tries to write and edit at the same time.

If you haven't done this before, understand there's more to self-editing than moving around your adjectives, adverbs and nouns.

Distilling a draft into a concise piece of writing takes some discipline and an ounce of self-awareness.

It's difficult to cut a paragraph or a chapter that you love… if it's not working out.

That said, it's also what most successful non-fiction authors do before they send their drafts to beta readers for review or to a professional editor for feedback.

GETTING READY TO EDIT YOUR FIRST DRAFT

After spending weeks or months writing about a topic, the work becomes too hot to touch, let alone edit.

When you finish your first draft, let it sit in your computer for a few days (or longer depending on the length of your book).

Swim. Run. Meditate. Eat steak in an expensive restaurant. Take the dog for an overdue walk. Do something that has nothing in common with writing.

Your ideas will cool and your memory fade. Later, when you open up that messy first draft, you'll look at it and think, "Oh yeah, I remember this."

Before you edit anything, change the line spacing of your work to double-spaced. Change the font to Courier New and the size to 12.

Better yet, download the font Courier Prime. This revised version of the Courier font looks better on larger screens and has all the benefits of its older brother.

(Available at https://www.fontsquirrel.com/fonts/courier-prime)

Many professional journalists and sub-editors format their work this way because it's easy on the eye and takes approximately one minute to read a page. This simplifies spotting errors, and you'll also have plenty of space for writing on your manuscript.

If you're submitting to an editor, you'll need to change the font back to double-spaced Times New Roman 12pt with one inch margins.

Font choice aside, print out your work, sit down at a quiet table and read your first draft in one go.

Confession: I feel guilty about the paper I use while self-editing, and I have great intentions to plant a small forest one day.

MARKING UP YOUR MANUSCRIPT

Don't feel disheartened if your first read-through disappoints.

The American editor Sol Stein likens the process of reviewing a first draft to performing triage on a patient, and that's what you're about to do with a red pen.

Strike through words with your pen, use arrows to move your sentences around, and write in the spaces between each sentence.

Your markups don't have to make sense to anyone but you. If you're in doubt about a change, circle the sentence or word with your pen, and decide on this edit later.

I sometimes read my work aloud and record myself using the voice memo app on my phone.

Then, I listen back to this recording and mark up the manuscript. The act of saying something aloud helps identify problems in a way my eyes can't.

Now that you have a sense of your manuscript, you're going to self-edit your book in at least three different ways.

Round 1: Editing the Structure of a Book Chapter

During this round, concern yourself with how you've organised your book chapter as a whole rather than the finer points of grammar.

For example, during this edit, I re-read the introduction and conclusion to see if they gel with each other.

Ask yourself:

- Does my introduction *invoke curiosity* in the reader?
- Do I invoke at least *one of the five senses* in each page of this chapter?
- Have I *cut the weakest part* of this chapter?
- Have I *included metaphors or similes* that, upon reflection, don't stand up?
- Have I used *compelling subheadings* so that my chapter is more readable?
- Do I need to *reformat my work* or source images?
- Am I *happy with the tone* of this chapter?
- Do I need to *interview* an additional source for this chapter?

- Can I *strengthen* my arguments by including facts, figures, quotes or third-party research?

Round 2: Editing Your Book Chapter in Relation to Other Chapters

Like a general surveying the battlefield before marshalling his troops, take stock of each book chapter in relation to the rest of *your book*.

Ideally, a book chapter falls naturally between the preceding and proceeding chapters. It also has a title and word count consistent with the rest of your book.

It's also sometimes pleasing to sign-post or reference different chapters in your book at this point too, i.e. "I'll talk more about this in Ch.5" and so on.

That said, be careful not to clear your throat so much that you distract your readers.

While editing *The Power of Creativity*, I stepped back and looked at my book as a whole. Then I dumped two unnecessary chapters and wrote a new one.

I was less concerned with pretty little sentences than with arranging my book in a way that agreed with readers. So address the big problems by asking yourself:

- Does the *central argument* of my book stand up?
- Does each chapter hold true to my book's *controlling idea*?
- Is each chapter of a *consistent length*?
- Are the chapters in the *right order*?
- Are the titles of my book chapters consistent with the *tone of my book*?
- Do I need to break my book up into *explicit sections*?
- Have I told an *emotional story* throughout my book that resonates with readers?

- Are the *central ideas or stories* within each chapter specific to these chapters alone or should I sign-post them elsewhere?
- Have I brought an *original insight* into my work?
- Have I checked the *introduction and conclusion* of each chapter so that it intrigues or satisfies readers?
- Do I repeat myself?
- What *metaphors, ideas and turns-of-phrase* do I overuse throughout the book?

Round 3: Line Editing Your Book Chapter

Line editing is like polishing your car. You can spend hours doing it and still not feel happy with how each line looks or your book sounds. That said, it helps to know the basics:

- **Use the active voice:** The chapter was edited by me. Oh dear. I hired an editor to fix my book. That's better.
- **Eliminate unnecessary words:** Look closely for unnecessary adverbs (there's one) and pointless adjectives (there's another).
- **Eliminate clichés** like your life depends on it.
- **Simplify clunky language:** My book, it is filled, with all manner of long sentences that must be edited down. I read these sentences aloud…. and cut them out.
- **Attributing dialogue?** Just say 'said': She gesticulates. He grimaces. We giggled. "That's not how people talk," your editor said.
- **Look for moments of lazy writing:** Do you make a living from your books? Or do you earn a living from your books?
- **Avoid using the same word over and over and over…:** The writing software Scrivener will help you find overused words. A thesaurus is useful too.
- **Kill your mixed metaphors:** Your readers are watching you like you're a hawk.

- **Avoid complicated language:** Your exasperated readers won't have the inclination to ruminate on your warblings.
- **Use suitable formatting:** Put key words in italics and bold, and break things up with lists, like this one.
- **Review your punctuation:** Unless you're tweeting like Donald Trump, cut those exclamation marks!
- **Love the comma:** "Let's eat, grandma." isn't quite the same as "Let's eat grandma."
- **And those dangling modifiers have to go:** You possibly include them because they simply sound good. And your reader's reaction? Really?!
- **In doubt?** Brevity is clarity. Cut 10% of your work.
- **Write compelling sub-headings:** Don't begin your work with a boring Introduction and end it with a stereotypical Conclusion.
- **Check your formatting**: Did you use compelling sub-headings and include images that add value to your book? Did you format your writing using bold, italics, block quotes, lists and so on?

What a line-edit by hand looks like

Hemingway App is a useful free tool that will help you eliminate clunky language and address many of the issues raised above.

GETTING HELP

Should you press enter once or twice after a paragraph? Is it better to refer to an interviewee by his or her first or last name? What's correct; etc. or ct cetera?

While self-editing a non-fiction book, it's natural to face questions like these and feel unsure about the right answer

So, let consistency be your North Star. If you wrote "etc." on page one, write "etc." on page 201. If you're still struggling, consider subscribing to a professional style guide like the *Chicago Manual of Style* or the *Harvard Style Guide*.

The authors of style guides like these have already faced and answered these questions many times. If you've got a troubling question, you can just look it up.

What's more, if you're self-publishing your book, you can refer your editor to these industry-standard guides, and he or she can root out any discrepancies for you.

(That said, sometimes it's good to break the grammar police's rules.... once it's a deliberate choice that improves rather than detracts from your book.)

PROOFING AND FACT-CHECKING YOUR WORK

Publishing your book with a typo or a factual mistake is like arriving at a party with your fly open.

Sure, some people will look away. But somebody's going to notice, and when they do, you're going to feel embarrassed.

So it's no wonder typos and bad grammar keep a lot of new authors up at night.

The longer you work on a book, the more likely you are to slip deeper into it and become blind to these typos and mistakes.

Now, you could obsess about typos and bad grammar and never go to that party at all. Mistakes appear in books of all types, even traditionally published ones with a large editorial budget. That's one reason publishers release second, third, fourth and revised editions of popular books.

For example, the first edition of the James Bond novel *Moonraker* by Ian Fleming contained a typo on page 10. The letter "t" was missing from the word "shoot". Today, that version is rather valuable.

Still, nobody wants to turn up to a party (or a bookstore) and embarrass themselves.

Them thar ttypos keep me up at night, so here's my checklist:

- Have you read your work out loud in a quiet place, listening for words that sound out of place?
- Did you check your work for your most common spelling and grammar mistakes?
- Are your figures correct, and do they add up?

- Did you spell your sources' names correctly and give them the appropriate titles?
- Have you cited all your sources?
- Do your links work? If you're editing a book for print, remember to type out the links.
- Did you check your grammar and spelling using Grammarly?

This list is a good start. But all of this will only take you so far, unfortunately. Proofreading is time-consuming, and because you're so close to your non-fiction book, you will inevitably overlook some mistakes.

I wasted a lot of time trying to proof my first book myself, only to have unhappy readers email me about some typos.

Giving chapters of your book to trusted friends and family is one workaround, and it shouldn't cost you much (beyond returning the favour!). However, be sure they're eagle-eyed.

That said, it pays to hire a proofreader, something I cover in a later chapter.

HOW MANY ROUNDS OF SELF-EDITING IS ENOUGH?

Great writing is rewriting.

You should self-edit your book at least three times: by sentence, by chapter and as a whole. That said, you can write, review, edit and rewrite your book many more times before it's good enough to publish.

Take it sentence by sentence, paragraph by paragraph and chapter by chapter. As you self-edit and write (but not at the same time!), your book will teach you how to finish writing it.

While working on your second or third draft, enlist the help of a family member or friend, and ask them to provide frank feedback.

Later on, enlist beta readers, a professional editor and a proofreader. Ask them to help you turn your self-edited draft into something you're proud to publish.

Working with editors, in particular, is the quickest way to master the self-editing process because they'll teach you things you just can't see.

Some writers rework their book until it goes to the printing press, and today thanks to self-publishing, you can even rewrite your work after publication.

But don't get stuck on a merry-go-round of self-editing your book without an end in sight.

Diminishing returns will set in. If you've taken the time to listen to your editor, you've done your job. So, accept that while your book isn't perfect, it's as good as can be.

And that's all your readers can ask.

YOUR WRITING EXERCISES

- Change the font of your writing to Courier New or Courier Prime, the line spacing to double and the size to 12. Now, print out your manuscript and mark it up.
- After atoning to the environment by planting a small forest, work through your manuscript at least three times. During each pass, edit a different part of your work.

PART III
FINDING LASTING SUCCESS WITH YOUR BOOK

ACTING ON CRITICAL FEEDBACK (WITHOUT LOSING YOUR MIND)

"Authors who moan with praise for their editors always seem to reek slightly of the Stockholm syndrome." – Christopher Hitchens

"Welcome to the team," said Deborah, shaking my hand. "It's my job to review all of your news stories and to give you topics to cover each week."

She was a tall, thin, blonde woman in her mid-thirties and the paper's news editor.

"You'll have to bear with me," I said. "I have a lot to learn about writing and journalism."

"I'm sure we'll figure things out, Bryan."

The first thing I figured out was how much everyone on the news team disliked Deborah, and I got right in line. She treated the three other news journalists like school children, even though we were in our mid-twenties.

One Tuesday morning, I was explaining to Emma, another news journalist, about how to find the contact details for a local politician.

Deborah glared across the office, snapped her fingers at us and said, "You two, get back to work."

"Deborah," I said. "We're talking about a news story."

"Well, hurry up. You have a deadline."

Deborah didn't like to see us talking to each other unless she was a part of the conversation. So we spent the rest of the day complaining about Deborah over instant messaging.

Deborah also liked to keep us working late in the office for no particular reason. I disliked her habit of interrupting my lunch break and ringing me at home or on my days off to ask for news updates and story ideas.

I started turning off my phone outside of hours and eating my lunch on another floor.

Events came to a head one Wednesday morning, the day after the weekly newspaper went to press. As soon as Emma, the rest of the journalists and I arrived into the office, Deborah began berating us in front of the rest of the newsroom.

"You're turning over half-finished stories way past your deadline," she said. "If you spent as much time working on your news stories as you do goofing off, we wouldn't have this problem."

"You've no right to talk to us like this, Deborah," said Emma. "Not in front of the entire office."

"Emma's right, Deborah," I said, feeling brave. "You can't treat us this badly… and there was nothing wrong with my story. I sent it on time, perhaps you should check your email."

"I've never met a group of more unprofessional and incompetent journalists," said Deborah.

"You have the nerve to call us unprofessional?" said Emma. "You treat us like school children."

"How dare you!" said Deborah.

"How dare you!" said Emma.

I thought they were going to come to blows, but the newspaper's managing editor stepped in and asked them to come into his office. They spent the rest of day thrashing things out in his office, his door closed and blinds pulled down.

My time came the following day. The editor asked Deborah to wait outside. Then, he pulled out a draft of my news story, which he had marked up with red pen.

"Can you see what's wrong with this story Bryan?" he said.

I scanned through his annotations. I had spelt a politician's name wrong, cited an incorrect figure and, worst of all, I had inadvertently insinuated a public figure was on the take.

My mistakes lined up on the page like rotten eggs.

"Deborah and I were here till 9 p.m. the night before last trying to fix these," he said. "If I let this go to print, we would have been sued, Bryan. You must double-check every name and triple-check every statistic and figure."

As much as I disliked Deborah and her management style, I couldn't blame these mistakes on her. I possessed too much self-belief in the veracity of my work.

So I started questioning every piece I worked on… and I started missing my deadlines because I was so worried about mistakes and getting negative feedback.

I went in search of rounded-out facts and perfect stories when Deborah (and later editors I worked with) wanted a piece on-time. They wanted articles that would stand up in the light of day.

My pendulum of self-belief swung from over-confidence in my work to self-doubt and procrastination. It took me years to find a centre point between the two.

WHY YOU MUST REGARD YOUR EDITOR AS AN ALLY (AND SEPARATE YOURSELF FROM YOUR WORK)

Your editor shouldn't be your friend, but they are on your side. They will help you get your book ready for your readers because that's their job. They're not going to waste their time or money on a writing project that won't sell (or which no one will read).

A book represents a business investment, and they want to see a return. Similarly, if you're self-publishing, your book is *an investment in your business*, and you should have the same mindset as an editor.

Now, you may think:

"What about art? What about my muse? What about writing for myself first?"

Well, I once spent a year writing a collection of short stories only to finish them and realise I had no idea who would want to read these stories. I hadn't written anything people would read, let alone pay for.

I learned the hard way to consider my ideal readers, what they enjoy and what they want before starting any writing project. That's what a good editor will do for you.

When you hire an editor, he or she should help you refine your book, so it speaks to one person rather than the masses. (That said, don't abdicate responsibility for your book's problems.)

Sending a manuscript to an editor is invigorating. But opening a Word document filled with annotations, comments and suggested changes feels like a frustrating step backward.

Many new writers brood about these slights and even feel sorry for themselves (I know because this is what I did). They let a marked-up manuscript sit in their computer for weeks or even months before doing anything with it.

That's a crucial mistake.

Here's why:

When a plumber fits a toilet, they don't view the toilet as an extension of themselves.

When a farmer milks a cow, they don't throw a temper tantrum if someone complains that the milk is sour.

So why should writing a non-fiction book be any different?

When an editor criticises your work, it's not personal. Their criticism is not a judgment on whether you're a good or bad person. Get some distance from your work, and you'll be able to evaluate your editor's advice on its merits alone.

Even if you're working with a publisher, your editor wants you to write a book their readers love and that earns their company a return.

On the other hand, if you're self-publishing, your editor will help you fix the problems in your book, but it's up to you to apply their advice. They've little to lose or gain if you publish a best-selling book or a turd. Either way, you'll have to pay for their services.

So when your editor asks for more research, a rewrite or suggests cutting a section, put your ego aside and listen.

These practical tips will help you handle critical feedback from your editor:

- Read through your editor's feedback and your marked-up manuscript in one go.
- If you're feeling confused, get out from behind your email, ring your editor and ask them questions.
- If you find their feedback tough to take, set your work aside for a day or two before returning to edit your book.
- Set yourself a deadline for working through your editor's feedback.
- Keep a copy of the old version of your work before you start editing. This way, you can undo changes if needed.
- Work on the proposed structural changes first, taking care to update your editor about what you're doing.
- Remember, you don't need to accept all of your editor's suggestions or changes.
- Next, fill in gaps in your research.
- Work through the suggested line edits.
- Send the revised draft back to your editor for another review, if needed.

GETTING FEEDBACK FROM BETA READERS

Musicians often demo early versions of their songs at smaller gigs to select audiences. They use their fans' feedback to improve these songs before recording and releasing them.

For your non-fiction book, find a group of early or beta readers you trust. Ask a more experienced colleague at work, an eagle-eyed family member who is great at catching typos, and readers of your blog or previous books (if you have them).

Many indie authors, for example, ask members of their email list to read their book before they publish it. Ask your beta readers:

- Did you spot any glaring typos or mistakes?
- Did you like the central story?
- Does the book's arguments (or controlling idea) stand up?
- Does the book deliver on its promise (your positioning statement)?
- Did you find any of the book confusing?
- What do you feel the book lacks?
- What should the book include more of?
- Is this book clear and concise?

An ideal beta reader will provide you with frank 'real-world' feedback you can use to improve your book before publishing it.

If your beta readers point out obvious mistakes, correct them, but don't let feedback become a reason for compromising on your entire work. After all, one person's Sistine Chapel is another person's trudge through a boring old church.

Part of becoming a professional author means having confidence in your ideas and your work. No, I'm not suggesting ignoring your beta readers altogether, but do have the courage of your convictions.

It's okay to disagree with your beta readers' feedback. Use a back-and-forth conversation to refine the confusing part of your book or to see if you can strengthen your controlling idea. Alternatively, set two rules for yourself:

- **Rule #1:** If at least one person likes a section in my book, it stays in.
- **Rule #2:** If three or more readers dislike a section in my book, I rewrite it.

After all, you're a professional.

WHAT YOU SHOULD KNOW ABOUT ADVANCED READER COPIES

Traditional publishers often send reviewers and those in the industry Advanced Reader Copies (ARCs) of a book before publication.

A beta reader will provide you with feedback about problems in your book (as you write it). Those receiving an ARC should get something close to the finished product, for example, a print copy of your book.

This approach is a great way of generating excitement about your book and soliciting reviews for the cover or inside of a book. It'll also help you unearth any remaining typos and mistakes.

EVERY AUTHOR NEEDS FEEDBACK

When I first started showing my writing to my mother/father/aunt/best friend, they'd tell me:

"It's great, Bryan. You've got talent."

I was like, "Wow, thanks. Writing for a living is my dream."

But their well-meaning feedback wasn't helpful. I needed someone like Deborah to tell me how it really was.

Now, Deborah and I didn't have a great working relationship. But she (and that newspaper editor) taught me one important lesson: *don't be precious about your work.*

I'm not going to lie to you.

Even today, getting editorial feedback is difficult, but I accept it as valuable medicine.

If you want to take your non-fiction book seriously and become a successful author, handling feedback, both good and bad, is part of the job.

Your internal critic should help you evaluate critical feedback. But don't let him or her prevent you from publishing your book.

Your editor should help you turn a page of lousy prose into something that shines, but know when to push back.

And your beta readers should help you improve your book so it satisfies them, but don't take everything they say as gospel.

Reading critical feedback sometimes feels like swallowing an oversized pill. Even though it's unpleasant, it's still a good idea to take your medicine.

So, get into the habit of putting what you learnt from editors, early readers and yourself into practice. Then, you'll spend less time fixing up first drafts and more time publishing books that readers love.

YOUR WRITING EXERCISES

- Send a second or third draft of a chapter in your book to at least three beta readers, and ask them for honest feedback.
- Spend 30 minutes each week reviewing what you've learnt from your editor and beta readers about the craft.

PICKING A BEST-SELLING TITLE FOR YOUR BOOK

"A good title is a work of genius. I have no hesitancy in saying that, for it is genius whether it is the inspiration of a lucky moment or the painful elaboration of a faint idea through an hour of deep thought." – Emanuel Haldeman-Julius

Emanuel Haldeman-Julius (1889-1951) found success by creating and publishing the *Little Blue Books* series of pamphlets, which sold 300 to 500 million copies in the United States and around the world. His company, Haldeman-Julius Publications, sold these books for a dollar, mostly through mail-order.

They sold various expired-copyright classics like the works of William Shakespeare alongside self-improvement books. If a book or pamphlet sold less than 10,000 copies in a year, Haldeman-Julius either withdrew the title from sale or took it into 'The Hospital'.

There, he often picked a more appealing title for the book in question and relaunched it. Here are several examples of title changes from The Hospital that increased sales:

- *The Mystery of the Iron Mask* sold 11,000 copies in a year,

while *The Mystery of the Man in the Iron Mask* sold over 30,000.
- *The King Enjoys Himself* sold 8,000 copies a year, but *The Lustful King Enjoys Himself* sold 38,000.
- *Ten O'Clock* sold 2,000 copies a year, while *What Art Should Mean To You* sold 9,000.
- *Art of Controversy* sold no copies, while *How To Argue Logically* sold 30,000.
- *Casanova and His Loves* sold 8,000 a year, but *Casanova, History's Greatest Lover* sold over 22,000.
- *Pen, Pencil and Poison* sold 5,000 a year, while *The Story of a Notorious Criminal* sold 15,800.

You want to sell more copies of your book, right?

Well, alongside selecting a great book cover, writing a captivating book title is one of your most important creative choices.

It's not much use having pretty sentences and great ideas, if your your title doesn't grab the attention of would-be readers.

BUT FIRST OFF...

Before writing your book title, be mindful of Amazon's rules for authors:

- The book title on your cover must match what your Amazon description says.
- You can't make claims about being a best-seller in your title.
- You can't claim deals, discounts or reduced prices in your title.
- No references to other books, authors or trademarks allowed.
- Your subtitle must be fewer than 200 characters.

Now that you know the rules, it's time to cover how to write a captivating book title.

STEP 1: RESEARCH RELATED POPULAR BOOK TITLES

Non-fiction authors traditionally pick self-explanatory book titles. Or they pick titles that rely on a central metaphor.

For example, Dale Carnegie wrote one of the most popular self-help books of all time: *How to Win Friends and Influence People*. Then, there's one of my favourites: Stephen King's non-fiction book *On Writing*.

You know almost immediately what both books are about from the titles alone.

Literary non-fiction writers traditionally pick book titles rich in resonance. They also pick titles that rely on a central metaphor from their books.

For example, consider Truman Capote's 1966 classic: *In Cold Blood*.

It's a non-fiction book about the murders of four members of the Herbert Clutter family in Kansas. This was a high-profile case in the 1960s, but you still need to read a little of Capote's book to discover what he's writing about.

A more recent example is Joan Didion's 2005 memoir: *The Year of Magical Thinking*.

It's an intriguing title, but it gives little away about the book. However, in the introduction, Didion explains the title encapsulates her year of intense grief after the death of her husband John Gregory Dunne.

For your own book, by now you should know the genre, who your ideal readers are and what books they read.

Now, *you can* pick an intriguing non-fiction book title that lends itself towards resonance. However, Capote, King and Didion are (or were) famous authors who could sell books on the strength of their names.

So why compromise?

Today, many successful non-fiction authors combine both approaches. They pick a title that invokes a central metaphor, and they also write a subtitle that sells the benefits of their book.

But before you do all that...

STEP 2: SUMMARISE WHAT'S IN IT FOR YOUR READERS

Consider Tim Ferriss's first book: *The 4-Hour Workweek: Escape 9-5, Live Anywhere, and Join the New Rich.*

In his book, Ferris explains how he uses outsourcing websites to simplify his life, but that's not in the sub-title. Instead, he sells readers on how they can escape the pain of the nine-to-five and follow their dreams.

To distil the benefits of your book, write down a list of five to ten things readers will understand or achieve by the end of your book. Focus on your readers' pain points and how your book will help them overcome these problems.

Use your subtitle to sell the pain.

Self-publishing expert and author Chandler Bolt gave me the following advice:

> It's easier to sell [painkillers] than it is to sell vitamins. When you're in pain, you whip out your credit card, and you will do anything to get out of pain. For vitamins we've got sugary ones, we've got gummy bears. We've got ones in shapes like fruit. It's so much harder to sell because it's not a basic need.

Features are your research, chapters, interviewees, ideas, word count and so on. Benefits, on the other hand, are what your readers *get out of your book*. They represent a problem-solved, kind of like painkillers.

STEP 3: WRITE YOUR BOOK TITLE AND SUBTITLE

Haldeman-Julius had two rules for writing a compelling book title. His first rule was to **make the title describe the book**. He explains:

> The title should contain some dominant word which clearly indicates the subject of the book. If it is biography or criticism, I think the title

should also indicate what the man stood for or what the matter criticised chiefly represents. If human nature can be put into the title, well and good. Every effort should be made to tie up the book with real life, or with the average person's desire for romance, adventure, and fun.

His second rule was to **make the title as distinctive as possible** "so as to compel attention and awaken interest."

PICKING THE RIGHT TITLE

Writing a clever metaphor or a title rich in meaning is tough work. You can simplify things by making a big claim in your title. Try and encapsulate your book's controlling idea in a few words, or make a promise to your readers.

Your title needs to convince people why they should read your book over all the other books clamouring for their attention. Of course, you must back up your claim or promise within your book too.

Dale Carnegie's big claim is clear: he'll teach you how to find more friends and persuade people.

PICKING THE RIGHT SUBTITLE

Your subtitle should be more specific and focus on benefits, rather than features. It should overcome objections potential customers have or be specific about your book's controlling idea.

Here is where hammer home what your book does.

EVALUATING YOUR TITLES

Go about writing ten or 20 variations of your title and subtitle. Ask yourself does each variation:

- Describe what the book is about?

- Explain what's in it for the reader?
- Bring different ideas together in fresh or distinctive ways?
- Consider what readers look for when they type in the names of books into stores like Amazon?

If you write and test multiple titles, you stand a better chance of writing one that grabs readers by the eyeballs.

STEP 4: OPTIMISE YOUR BOOK TITLE FOR SEARCH

Haldeman-Julius would have loved the powerful tools authors can use today to find out what readers search for.

The trick is to identify search terms or keywords and work them into your title, subtitle or book description. Once you do, you should attract more clicks to your sales page and sell more copies of your book.

"According to our statistics, the book that ranks number one for a search term gets 27% of the clicks. The book that ranks number two gets only 13% of the clicks," says author and SEO expert Dave Chesson.

"If you truly want to show up for that keyword, you either need to add it to your subtitle or put it in your description."

The good news is there are lots of free and paid tools that can help you do this.

GOOGLE KEYWORD PLANNER

To use this tool, you must sign up to a Google AdWords account, but it's free.

Google Keyword Planner will generate hundreds of search terms based on your topic. You can filter these by search volume and competition. You can also export your results to a spreadsheet and use this information to inform your title or subtitle.

A DEDICATED SEO TOOL

If you're publishing on the Amazon Kindle Direct Publishing (KDP) platform, you'll have to select seven keywords about your book.

SEO expert, Dave Chesson, says the best approach is to find seven or more popular, relevant keywords and use at least one of these in your title or subtitle.

"When I've nailed those seven, I [ask] which one of those seven is the best representation of my book?" says Dave.

You can find the best keywords using an SEO tool for authors like KDP Rocket.

These tools enable you to find popular search terms or keywords and check the popularity of relevant books.

"I will go ahead and put those seven [keywords] into KDP...but I'll also try to weave them into the subtitle," says Chesson.

STEP 5: TEST YOUR BOOK TITLE

It's easier today to test your book titles *before* publishing your book. If you make the wrong decision about your book title, you can always retest your choices and start again.

LET AMAZON HELP YOU

You can find popular book search terms in Amazon for your genre by typing in a few words into the search bar and letting Amazon auto-populate it for you.

Go to Amazon and type in 'How to' plus '[your book's topic]', and you'll immediately see related book titles that rank highly on Amazon.

Keep a swipe file of popular book titles related to your genre or topic and add to this over time.

Alternatively, study the most popular titles in your niche by using Amazon. It will recommend other titles based on what readers bought on the various sales pages and even via email. This information is a gold mine if you're self-publishing.

ASK YOUR READERS

If you have a mailing list of readers or you're working with beta readers, you could poll them using Google Forms or SurveyMonkey.

USE ADS

Tim Ferriss used Google AdWords to test titles for his first book. His preferred choice was *Broad Bends and White Sands* but after running an ad, he found readers preferred *The 4-Hour Workweek*.

Today, you can test book titles using Facebook ads.

Create two Facebook ads, each one based on a different book title. Then, target these ads at would-be readers of your book or fans of your author page. Let these run for three to five days, and see which one attracts the most clicks or likes.

For this to work, you'll need a modest budget (say $5 a day), a mockup of your book cover(s) and some understanding of how to create and track ads.

RUN A POLL

Once you have two or three book titles you like, you can run a poll. This is a great way of getting instant market feedback. You can post on a relevant Facebook group or use a premium service like PickFu.

I used the latter to A/B test two book titles, and I got more than 100 responses explaining why one title was more compelling than another. This feedback helped me improve the title in question.

CAPTURING THE ATTENTION OF BOOK BUYERS

Crafting a book title is one of your most important creative choices. You need a good title that convinces book buyers to click through to your sales page, download a sample and buy your book.

Now, non-fiction authors today can research and test book titles using tools that Haldeman-Julius and others would have loved.

So, find the middle ground between writing a title that does your book justice and one that readers will search for or remember.

YOUR WRITING EXERCISES

- Keep a list of popular non-fiction book titles you like. If you add to this list over time, then you'll train your brain into understanding what titles sell and don't sell, and you'll have a list you can consult while writing your title.
- Test your book title by running a poll, by asking your beta-readers for their opinions or by creating a Facebook ad.

SELF-PUBLISHING YOUR NON-FICTION BOOK LIKE A PRO

"Writing is about you. Publishing is about the book. Marketing is about the reader." – Joanna Penn

I still get a kick every time I upload a digital book file to Amazon and press publish. It's easy, and it's free... or is it?

Well, you could finalise a draft today. You could prepare your digital book file, knock up a masterpiece of a book cover in Paint (oh, my eyes, it burns!), upload it all to Amazon and have a book for sale within hours.

But should you?

Well, professional non-fiction authors take care to create books that readers love. They work with trained editors, professional designers and more. If you're self-publishing your non-fiction book and you take your craft and readers seriously, you should too.

So how much does it cost to self-publish a book?

According to the *Write Life*, the average amount a writer spends on self-publishing a book falls between $200 and $300. While according to *Book Promotion*, more experienced writers spend several thousand dollars on self-publishing services.

I've spent less than $500 and more than $2000 on self-publishing different books. There are advantages and disadvantages to working on a shoe-string and a larger budget.

I researched the pricing information in this chapter during 2017 and updated it before publication.

Some of the prices may have increased since then, but my advice about *what to budget for* holds true.

Let's dive in.

PAYING FOR WRITING AND SELF-PUBLISHING SOFTWARE

Whether you're self-publishing your book or otherwise, you still need a computer. You also need writing software like Google Docs, Word or Scrivener.

Once you've written your book, you can either hire a designer to prepare your digital book files or do it yourself. It's easy enough if you learn Scrivener's advanced features or use book design software like Vellum (Mac only).

Costs
Free to $74

For Authors on a Tight Budget
I'll presume you already own or have access to a computer for writing. At the back of this book, I include a list of free and premium writing software you can use.

A license for software like Scrivener and Vellum costs $45 and $29, respectively. If you can't afford to spend this modest amount on writing software, you're in the wrong game.

HIRING AN EDITOR, COPYEDITOR AND PROOFREADER

Almost every author works with a developmental editor, a proofreader and sometimes a copyeditor or line editor.

A developmental editor will provide critical feedback about the tone and direction of your book in the form of a reader's report. He or she may also provide some light copywriting, depending on your contract.

A copyeditor or line editor will go through each sentence and polish them for you. They will also check that your spelling, word-choice and the overall style of your book is consistent.

A proofreader will eliminate typos and grammar mistakes and may also look for factual inaccuracies.

Some editors also provide developmental and copyedits if you pay extra.

MY EXPERIENCES WORKING WITH EDITORS AND PROOFREADERS

While self-publishing my first book, *A Handbook for the Productive Writer,* I hired a proofreader, but I didn't hire an editor.

Having worked as a journalist and sub-editor, I felt confident about editing a non-fiction book myself. I also turned several chapters into guest blog posts for various websites. Later on, I used critical feedback from these editors to improve my book.

Even though their feedback was helpful, self-editing my book took dozens of hours, and I sprouted grey hairs out the back of my ears.

That wasn't my only mistake.

I hired a cheap proofreader for $200 to check *The Savvy Writer's Guide to Productivity*. This proofreader found some errors (but not all of them) in the book before I self-published it.

Then, after I uploaded the first version of my book, I found some additional errors and typos (the shame!).

After a reader complained to me about some typos, I rained furious hellfire down upon him. When that didn't work, I used the online proofreading service Grammarly to recheck every chapter. Then, I resent this book to a professional proofreader for $300.

A month after self-publishing the first version of my book, I uploaded a new version to Amazon.

I called it Version 2.

Later, I paid to have much of the book re-edited. I also retitled it as *The Savvy Writer's Guide to Productivity*. And I recovered the book so I could position it to the right readers more effectively and increase sales.

For every book since, I've worked with an editor, proofreader and occasionally a line editor.

Typically, an editor sends me a reader report with an annotated version of my manuscript. The proofreader and line editor also make changes in a document and send it back for me to accept or reject.

Feedback like this, while sometimes tough, improves the quality of my books and teaches me more about writing (a nice added bonus).

Now, you can hire an editor, proofreader and copyeditor based on:

- Your total word count
- The hours you want the editor/proofreader to spend on your book
- Your total page count
- Your project as a whole

Before hiring an editor or proofreader, ask them:

- What style they'll use? The Chicago Manual of Style is pretty popular.
- Will they edit your book in British or US English?
- Can they provide a sample edit for you to review (usually free)?
- Do they specialise in any type of writing?
- Can they provide testimonials from satisfied clients?
- How long will an edit take?
- What are their rates?

Costs

I don't have an easy answer for you because it depends on how clean your draft is, your subject matter and what level of editorial support you want. Rates vary widely too, so shop around.

That said... you can hire an editor and also a copyeditor for $40 to $50 per hour, each.

You can also expect to pay an editor and a proofreader $5 to $10 per 1000 words, each.

For Authors on a Tight Budget

If you can't afford an editor or proofreader, start saving! Working with an editor is the single best way to improve your book and your craft.

That said, joining a creative writing group or class is a great way to get free feedback on your writing. All you have to do is provide other people feedback on their work too. So the only real cost is your time.

Similarly, if you write guest blog posts based on your draft, you can get free editorial feedback about your non-fiction. After your guest post goes live, you can always reuse elements of the post as chapters in your book (with some light rewriting).

I caution against self-publishing your book without hiring or getting an eagle-eyed friend to proofread your book.

Those typos will come back to haunt you.

FINDING A CAPTIVATING BOOK COVER

Picking a good book cover is one of your most important creative decisions. It's your book's best chance of standing out against the hundreds of thousands of other books on stores like Amazon.

When I was starting off, I stayed up till two a.m. for nights on end taking online design tutorials. I created a cover that had almost nothing to do with the contents of my book.

Since then, I've run competitions on sites like 99designs and worked directly with book cover designers.

As an author, your time is better spent writing than it is tinkering in Photoshop or Illustrator. So either start saving or reframe the expense as an investment in your craft.

Hiring a Designer

It's relatively easy to find a professional book cover designer, and I've included resources at the back of this book. So find a designer you can afford who has experience creating book covers in your niche.

Then, you'll need to determine if he or she is free to work on your cover and then come to an agreement on price and deliverables. Some budget-friendly designers will let you pick from various book cover templates. More expensive designers will create something new for you.

Before you pay your designer, let them know if you want a front cover for digital publishing, a full cover for print and a 3D mockup of your book for your website.

These extras cost more. Also, insist on the source files (that's the Photoshop or Illustrator files and not just the book cover image), so you can edit the book cover later if necessary.

Decide on Your Budget

You can spend a lot or a little on your book cover. If you spend a modest amount (less than $100), you'll probably have to pick from various pre-designed templates. If you spend more, you can work one-on-one with a designer.

Do Your Research

The covers of thriller books look different from the covers of self-help books. The former relies on dark imagery, while the latter relies on hopeful imagery.

So, spend at least an hour browsing stores like Amazon and saving book covers in your niche that you like (Pinterest and Evernote are both good for this).

Write a Design Brief

If you've commissioned a new cover rather than using a pre-designed template, write a short brief for your designer. Explain what your book is about, the title, key concepts, what book covers you like/dislike and so on.

Are you okay with stock imagery? Do you prefer simple designs, or do you have an image in mind? Are there particular colours and fonts you like?

If your writing draws on key imagery or metaphors, let your designer know as they could work an element into your cover. Include a sample chapter for them to read too.

Providing this information will reduce the amount of time both of you spend going backwards and forwards about a design later.

Give Proactive Feedback

Depending on how much you pay, your designer will go through one or two rounds of changes with you. Tell them what you like and dislike about the cover, and what you want changed.

Remember, your book cover needs to look good at small sizes so it stands out in digital book stores.

But what if you don't know what you like? Ask a friend or your early readers for their opinions about the book cover. They may have a good eye for design or captivating images.

Crowdsourcing Your Book Cover

Sites like 99designs, CrowdSpring and DesignCrowd enable you to run competitions. If you host one, designers will submit covers for you to review. When you pick the best one, the winner gets a prize that you front.

I used 99designs in the past for a book cover, and I was happy with the results.

Two years ago, I wrote an article about my experiences. Some unhappy designers complained in the comments about crowdsourcing websites. They argued losers get nothing for their submission or hard work.

If you decide on this approach, you'll still need to brief your designer and work with the winner to finalise it.

Costs

It costs $50 to $500 or more to hire a designer, and as with hiring an editor, you get what you pay for. Competitions on crowdsourcing websites start at $240.

Preparing a Print Version of Your Book

What writer doesn't want to hold their book in their hands? If you follow the guidelines on Amazon and CreateSpace, you can do just that. Vellum (Mac only at time of writing) also enables writers to compile print version of their book.

If you can't or don't want to use Vellum, I recommend hiring a designer to prepare your print book. They will take care of headaches like laying out each page correctly. They will also check that your cover is the right depth, break up run-on sentences and so on.

Costs

It costs about $250 to $300 to hire a designer to prepare a 40,000 to 50,000 word book for print. I expect this cost to come down as self-publishing software becomes easier to use.

At time of writing, Vellum Press (for creating print books) costs $249.

For Authors on a Tight Budget

Yes, you could design a cover yourself in Paint or Photoshop or buy a cheap cover for a couple of dollars on a site like Fiverr. You could also rub lemons in your eyes, but that doesn't mean you should.

Unless you've got ace design skills, don't – a cheap cover screams cheap writing. If you can't afford to hire a designer, Canva provides a series of free ebook cover templates that you can adapt. Later on, you can always swap this cover for a more professional design.

There's no cheap shortcut to preparing a book for print, unfortunately. You can always prepare your book file using Vellum, but you'll need the help of a designer to get the cover right for print. If that's an issue, publish a digital copy of your book first and a print copy later on.

THE BOTTOM LINE

Authors today don't have to ask for permission from publishers, editors or even readers! However, you still need the funds to create a great book.

It cost me around $500 to self-publish my first book, $1000 to self-publish my second and over $2000 to self-publish my third.

In each case, I hired more expensive editors, designers and so on to improve the quality of the books in question. I also haven't included extra costs like what I spent on marketing my book using Facebook ads.

You can spend as much or as little as you want self-publishing your non-fiction book.

If you invest a little money, you'll break even on the cost of your book faster. But if you invest more, you'll create a better product and improve your craft with the help of a professional.

Unlike years ago, you're in control of your creative choices (including the budget), and that's a liberating place to be for most non-fiction authors.

YOUR WRITING EXERCISES

- Create a file of book covers from your niche that you like. Add to this file as you go, and show it to your designer.
- Decide up front how much you want to spend on editing, design and so on. Work within your budget, taking care to create a professional product (yes, books are products!) that readers love.

FINISHING (AND SHIPPING) YOUR BOOK

"It all sounded great in the script, and it was doable – just a matter of reps, reps, reps." – Arnold Schwarzenegger

When Arnold Schwarzenegger (b1947) was a teenager, he started lifting weights in the Athletic Union in Graz, Austria.

On the wall next to where they lifted weights, each athlete listed exercises like 'Dead Lift', 'Bench Press', 'Clean and Jerk, 'Shoulder Press' and so on. The athletes chalked a row of hash marks next to each exercise, each one representing a set.

After an athlete completed the reps comprising a set, they marked an X through the first line. To complete a session, the athletes, including Schwarzenegger, had to mark an X through each of the five or six lines.

In his biography *Total Recall*, Schwarzenegger writes:

> This practice had a huge impact on my motivation. I always had the visual feedback of 'Wow, an accomplishment. I did what I set out to do. Now I will go for the next set, and the next set.'

Schwarzenegger applied this mentality of completing reps and sets to find success as a bodybuilder and actor. He even completed his 'reps' to campaign for Governor of California.

There's a famous scene in *Terminator 2* where Schwarzenegger drives down a Los Angeles drainage canal on a Harley. He pulls out a shotgun, fires it, spins and re-cocks the weapon, fires again and so on, until he reaches a chained gate with a padlock. Then, the Terminator shoots the gates and drives through.

Schwarzenegger practiced using a weapon and bike for this scene hundreds of times for weeks beforehand. He worked through his reps and sets so much that he tore the skin off his fingers. He writes:

> I couldn't wear a glove because it would get stuck in the gun mechanism, and I tore the skin off my hand and fingers practicing a hundred times until I mastered the skill.

While governor of California, Schwarzenegger prepared for a big campaign speech by renting a studio. There, he visualised his audience. Schwarzenegger delivered his speech over and over for three days. Each time, he marked his reps on the front page.

If you're worried your book isn't good enough, work through your reps. Schwarzenegger bled into his stunts, and you can bleed into your first lines, books and your craft.

The more sentences you write, the stronger your command of the language will become. The more clichés you terminate, the better you'll become at editing.

The more chapters you write, the better you'll be at articulating stories and ideas. And the more books you finish, the more you'll know about how to write the next one.

And the next.

And the next.

I'M WORRIED THEY'LL JUDGE ME

In December 2016, a friend asked me to help with a street collection for a charity in Dublin. Being introverted, I procrastinated about it for two weeks before agreeing. Then, I donned a luminous bib for the charity, and I wandered out onto the rainy, cold streets.

I held out the bucket as strangers walked up and down the street. They looked at their phones, their shoes, ahead, behind me. They looked anywhere and everywhere but at me and my half-empty bucket.

(I couldn't blame them. I've done the same many times.)

I was jingling the coins inside the bucket and studying a billboard for a new *Star Wars* film when a well-dressed middle-aged woman tapped me on the shoulder.

"I want you to know why I can't donate today," she said, her voice round like an over-sized lemon. "They organised a big collection at church on Sunday, and I gave a lot, *a lot*."

"That's good to know," I wrapped my hands around the bucket. "I best get back to it."

The woman nodded, pulled her handbag onto her shoulder and walked down the street.

That night, I wondered why this well-heeled woman was so concerned about what I thought of her refusal to put a few euro into my lonely bucket.

(I wasn't even thinking about her!)

Many new writers worry their audience will judge them or what people close to them will think of their book or creative works. So they look away from the page, and they hold something back from their book.

I get it. I do it too.

Those messy personal stories – the party where I drank too much, called the host the wrong name and passed out in the bathroom. Or the time they fired me because my maths weren't up to the task. Those don't frighten me. I know how those stories turn out. It's telling you about them. I care too much about what you think.

Many writers worry their readers will judge them.

Last year, I was 100 pages into a non-fiction book by a *New York Times* best-selling author. I was enjoying the author's way with words until he teased a personal story.

He told his readers about a time of inner crisis, only to announce it was too personal to reveal. Then he promptly moved on without revealing anything more. I threw his book across the room.

What was the point in reading on?

This author, as accomplished as he is, was too worried that his readers would judge him. Well, your readers want to know they're not alone. They need you to share some essential truth from your life with them.

In a world of click-bait, fake news and cute cat videos, they crave authenticity. So instead of worrying they'll judge you, be as honest as you can.

I FEEL STUCK

Finishing is harder than starting.

When I was in my mid-twenties, I spent years struggling to finish anything. I wrote dozens of short stories and abandoned them. I researched articles I wanted to write for newspapers, and then I never wrote them.

There wasn't any one moment when I learnt how to finish my work. Instead, I got a job as a journalist writing for a newspaper. There, I had to finish my articles by a deadline because if I didn't, the editor would fire me.

I know this because he called me into his office after I missed a deadline and said so. So I stopped polishing my articles until they were perfect and I finished them.

On more than one occasion, my editor sent articles back to me, saying I'd left out an important paragraph or my introduction needed reworking.

After listening to his criticism, I wanted to quit.

On other occasions, the sub-editors of the paper reworked my articles. This process felt like a brutal dressing-down, but at least I was getting paid to write.

If you're having trouble, act like a professional.

- Set artificial deadlines for each chapter, and stick to them.
- Tell your editor or readers you'll have a draft ready by the end of the day/week/month, and keep your promise.
- Create a book sales page on Amazon, upload your cover and write the sales copy. Then, set a realistic publication date.

The chapters you finish are akin to the threads of a cable, and you'll weave them together day by day until your work is secure.

Then, you'll have more opportunities to gain feedback about your book. In turn, you'll gain the confidence you need to finally finish it.

WHAT IF I FAIL?

So the reviews are in.

So your work sucked.

So your book wasn't any good.

Accept it. Move on.

I don't mean to be harsh.

If you're anything like me or other writers I've met, you'll have far more failures to your name. You'll have more unpublished disasters on your computer than five-star books. And you'll know more about disappointment than success.

I failed to build a career as a news journalist. I failed to hold down a well-paying contract with a magazine I read. I failed to turn a well-paying freelance job into a profitable permanent job.

Worst of all, I failed to write and publish a book before I was 30 (a life-long goal).

Failure – it's tough.

On good days, I felt restless, and on bad days I felt depressed by my lack of progress.

Writing is a personal thing, and not something you can fake or dial in. If you want to finish writing your book and become a successful non-fiction author, you'll fail many times before you get there.

Instead of wallowing in self-defeat, salvage what you can, and use the experience as a lesson to fall forwards. Failure and rejection are pit stops along your journey to becoming a better writer.

Wondering if you've got what it takes, blaming your editor and suffering from a martyr complex won't help you write a better book next time. Feedback is invaluable. It's your chance to learn how to become a better writer for free.

English author Neil Gaiman says:

> Whatever it takes to finish things, finish. You will learn more from a glorious failure than you ever will from something you never finished.

When you publish a book, your career gains momentum. You become a creative professional who can think of an idea, flesh it out, edit, rewrite, polish and rewrite some more, before finally pressing publish.

That takes guts.

WHAT IF I SUCCEED?

One new writer emailed me to say she worried what would happen if her book was a success and she became famous. She said:

> I want to tell stories, and I want people to read them and get joy and satisfaction from them, I just don't want to become a subject under a microscope!

I get it. Publishing a book can feel like you're walking out onto the street wearing no pants.

Will people treat you differently? How will you react when they talk about the stories you told? And will this change you?

Yes, your imagined answers to these questions may feel embarrassing, but your real problem isn't what people think. It's getting their attention in the first place.

The prospects of becoming Malcolm Gladwell—famous for your work are slight. That said, it's natural to worry how those around you will react to your book.

It's normal to wonder what will happen if you become known for being an author.

If you succeed, you'll discover a new side to yourself and your craft, which will only enrich your life. It's impossible to please everyone, so if some people feel uncomfortable with your success, that's their problem.

After all, you will regret not having the courage to see your ideas and your book through later. So hold onto your values, and finish writing your book.

At the very least, you'll be able to afford some new pants or a gym membership.

Schwarzenegger would be proud.

KNOW WHEN YOU'RE AT THE END

Most people spend more time telling their friends they have this great idea for a book than they do turning their vision into reality.

If you've made it this far and finished your book, you're a different kind of writer.

Look:

There will always be a gap between what you want your non-fiction book to achieve and what comes out on the blank page.

The best way to narrow that gap and improve the quality of your book is to put in your reps:

Write more often, finish your book and publish it.

If you've come this far, you're in the minority. It takes a tremendous amount of hard work and mental discipline to release the best possible version of your non-fiction book into the world.

But when you're done, you're done.

Congratulations!

YOUR WRITING EXERCISES

- Work through your reps each day. Practice free writing. Practice headline writing. Practice editing your book. It all counts.
- Free write for 10 to 15 minutes about what your finished book (this book, not another one!) will do for your career/craft/readers. Now, do all you can to turn your vision into a reality.

FREE, FREE AT LAST!

"Life's as kind as you let it be." – Charles Bukowski

So you've finished writing your book, and you're about to release it to the world. It's an exciting and scary place to be.

Should you quit your job, wait for the royalties to flow into your bank account, retreat to the Bahamas and write full-time on a hammock? Or should you strike writing a book off your bucket list and move on with your life?

Well, before you come to any big decisions, wait.

It's always a wise move to ask yourself, "What does success looks like?" Once you publish your book, you're free to decide what happens next.

For some new authors, it's enough to write one book and move on with their lives. Other new authors want to earn a return and even a living from their books and quit their day jobs.

Then, there are authors who care more about reaching as many people as possible with their ideas than they do about their bank accounts.

In this chapter, I'll explain what freedom for most non-fiction authors looks like. I'll also cover what you can expect now that you've finished writing your first non-fiction book.

(Oh, and congratulations by the way!)

WHEN FREEDOM MEANS WRITING FOR THE LOVE OF YOUR CRAFT

I spent almost every Monday in 2007 taking writing classes in Dublin city centre. Twelve of us met every Monday in an airy room overlooking a small park full of old winos near O'Connell Street.

"I'm going to teach you all about great literary non-fiction," said the instructor on the first day of class. He was a balding Texan who took the craft more seriously than his students did. "But first, tell me why you are all here."

"To learn how to write one, true sentence," said a student.

The instructor nodded.

"I have a painful story from my past, and I'm going to write a book about it," said a second student.

The instructor stroked his goatee and smiled.

Perhaps we were all right after all.

"I want to become a rich and famous writer," said a third student.

The instructor's face turned a pale shade of yellow.

"I don't think this class is for you." He stood. "I'm going to give your money back. Please take your things and go."

The student's mouth opened and closed like a flapping seal. Then, he put his notepad in his bag, stood, collected €250 from the teacher and left us to it.

I thought about that moment for years afterwards. I thought about it when I was finishing one terrible literary non-fiction essay after the next, at home alone, again.

I'm just trying to write a great sentence! This is what the craft is all about.

So I gave it a minute.

I gave it five years.

And I got impatient.

Impatient? Yes. But I was in my twenties. I could have done with some advice from Natalie Goldberg, who said:

> Play around. Dive into absurdity and write. Take chances. You will succeed if you are fearless of failure.

Eventually, I learnt not every author wants to earn a full-time living from their book.

While getting paid is nice, lots of authors have well-paying jobs and prefer to write a book around the margins of the day. They want to write without expectation or pressure to succeed.

You could have a story you want to tell and have no desire to go at it full-time. For you, freedom means getting your book out into the world.

That's okay!

What a relief to not worry about shifting copies and creating related products and services, and earning a return on your creative work.

Now, you can concentrate on writing your next book, or you can learn to play *Hey, Soul Sister* on the ukulele.

It's your choice.

I also thought about that moment from the writing class when I looked at my dwindling bank account at the end of the month (I'm conflicted like that).

Why am I spending so much time on something that almost never pays? Shouldn't I spend my time swatting up on investment funds, short selling and currency trades?

Almost no author earns a living from writing literary non-fiction, and I am no exception. Much later, I barely broke even on my first book. I only learnt how to earn an income from the blank page after studying book marketing and copywriting.

But all that writing for free taught me more about the craft than any paycheque ever could.

You see, if your non-fiction book is a labour of love, its existence is a success. You've done more than the thousands of writers who sit in bars and coffee shops, telling their friends.

"I've got a great idea for a book, I just need to actually write it!"

You've listened to the inner muse whispering, *Write, damn it!*

That takes guts.

WHEN FREEDOM MEANS EARNING AN INCOME

My first gig as a professional journalist paid just €100 a day. That's barely enough to cover the cost of childcare, petrol and lunch.

"I can't live on this," I said to my editor. "What's a starving writer supposed to do?"

"Bryan, I've heard that one before," he said. "There are dozens of resumes on my desk from journalism graduates like you."

The sad thing is he was right. I was only starting off, and I couldn't expect a large paycheque. I thought my work would stand for itself and bring in the big bucks.

I spent most of my twenties arguing marketing and writing have almost nothing in common and that my time was best spent writing.

Funny coincidental fact:

I spent most of my early twenties struggling to earn a living as a professional writer.

Was this because my peers were more talented than I was?

At the time, I thought so. Now, I know they were better at telling stories about their work and forming connections with new editors, readers and clients. They marketed themselves and their work, and they got paid for doing it.

A doctor gets paid for attending to their patients, a plumber for installing a shower and even a chiropodist for lopping off those awful bunions.

You can get paid as well.

One book isn't going to earn you a Stephen-King-sized paycheque. According to a Digital World Book Survey, a typical Kindle author earns about $50 to $999 per year. And, according to a 2016 Author

Earnings report, most indie authors earn approximately $100 per title.

That's not a lot to show for the time and money you spent on your book. To earn a living from your writing, you must develop lots of income streams.

Getting Paid for Writing Books

Take note of the plural heading.

If you're committed to a career as a non-fiction author, starting on the next book is the best marketing and creative decision you can make.

Each time you write a book, you're putting in your reps, building a body of work and improving your craft. When you publish your new book, you'll increase sales of your old books because readers have more opportunities to find your work.

Better yet, you could turn your non-fiction book into part of a series. Indie author Joanna Penn earns a six-figure income from her writing and has published a series of popular *books* for writers.

Then there's professor Yuval Noah Harari whose work *Sapiens* was one of the most popular non-fiction books of 2014. So in 2016, he published a sequel *Homo Deus: A Brief History of Tomorrow*.

Caveat: you still need to take time out from writing to market your books and connect with existing and new readers.

Getting Paid for Your Services

Henneke Duistermaat is a successful copywriter. She self-published a series of books about content marketing and copywriting. She's also drawn upon her experiences to write guest posts for popular sites that her clients read.

"I got all my first clients through guest posting," says Henneke. "I looked for popular blogs that were read by small business owners and business people. I wrote blog posts for them about copywriting."

Getting Paid to Teach

Danny Iny is a teacher and writer who publishes on Amazon short books about his insights. He's a master of turning the information in his books into premium courses for his readers.

Typically, teachers like Danny give their books away for free (or at a steep discount) and sell their courses anywhere from $47 to $3,000.

Getting Paid for Coaching Clients

I met a marketing consultant who sells her book about content strategy on Amazon for several dollars. It has dozens of five-star reviews, but she doesn't rely on her Amazon earnings to earn a living.

Instead, she charges corporations tens of thousands of dollars for teaching the principles in her book to executives. Her non-fiction book is her business card.

Getting Paid for Writing What the Market Wants

Steve Scott is a prolific non-fiction author from the United States. He writes and publishes short non-fiction books for $2.99. Each of these are 10,000 to 20,000 words long, and he publishes one every few months. His titles include:

- *The Miracle Morning for Writers: How to Build a Writing Ritual That Increases Your Impact and Your Income (Before 8AM)*
- *How to Write Great Blog Posts That Engage Readers*
- *How to Start a Successful Blog in One Hour*

Specific. Concise. Profitable.

WHAT DOES FREEDOM LOOK LIKE FOR YOU?

Look, there's a time for being alone in the room and doing the work. There's also a time for telling stories about your book and building connections with other writers, readers and editors.

Successful non-fiction authors who earn a decent living do all these things. They spend time writing, researching and promoting their books. And they also find out what their readers and editors want.

The copywriter wants to attract new, high-paying clients for her business. So she publishes a book about her speciality, prices it for $4.99 and provides details of her services in the book. She cares less about recognition for her literary prowess than she does about attracting leads.

The blogger wants to entertain and inspire thousands of readers around the world. So he publishes a book for $2.99.

He knows that'll barely keep him drinking Mocha Frappucinos, but he doesn't care. He writes for other sites and magazines for free to build his profile. And when he gets a little bigger, he considers coaching some of his readers or even offering them an online course.

The indie author wants to quit her job and write full time. She studies what the market wants and writes her book accordingly.

She knows it's the first part of a series and that it takes a backlist to become a well-paid indie author. She also knows what she's passionate about, and the best way to sell the last book is to write the next one.

The student in a literary writing class regards success as getting his non-fiction story out of his head and onto the blank page.

So he polishes his work until it shines. He submits a few chapters to literary magazines and gets his book published. Then, he either tries again or moves on with his life, after ticking writing a book off his bucket list.

As a new author, you have all you need to answer what freedom means for you. You can turn your vision into a reality.

YOUR WRITING EXERCISES

- What drives you: earning an income, making an impact or

writing for the love of your craft? Use your answer to frame what you write next.
- Until your writing is earning you a decent income, don't quit your job. Instead, regard the 9-to-5 as a crutch that supports your writing.

THE END

We tell ourselves we'll do the work and write a non-fiction book, but often we don't. We put it off until tomorrow. We fuss about our ideas. We worry about not having enough time.

But now, you know better.

In a few months, you could be holding a copy of your finished book in your hands.

Yes, it's hard work. But once you're done, you'll be free to start writing another book. Or you can attract new clients and customers. Or you can even take a break from the craft of book-writing.

Because when you take an idea, turn it into a first draft, edit your work and publish like a professional author, you're free to decide what happens next.

If you want to sell your book, you should go out and tell readers stories about it. Tell them what your book is about. Tell them whether it entertains, inspires, educates or informs.

If you commit to a career as a non-fiction author, start another one... and soon. You can spend a lifetime learning to improve your craft, discovering what readers want and learning how to sell books.

As a committed non-fiction author, you're never really done – you're just out of time.

Now, so am I.

THE TEN COMMANDMENTS FOR SUCCESSFUL NON-FICTION AUTHORS

Behold:

1. **Thou shalt commit to writing thy book,** for the writer who talks about the beginnings of a book and yet never fills the page shall be cast out.

2. **Thou shalt have a plan.** In the beginning, there was a controlling idea, an outline and a deadline. And it was good.

3. **Thou shalt always be researching,** for ideas are the currency of thy realm and thou art richer than thy wildest dreams.

4. **Thou shalt honour thy reader** for theirs are the problems thy book must solve. Theirs is the boredom thy book must alleviate. Theirs is the soul thy book must inspire.

5. **Thou shalt not covet a better writing tool or for tomorrow to come.** Abandon ye the error of your procrastinating ways and tremble! Thou must fill the blank page today and thou doth possess all thy need.

6. **Thou shalt learn to love thy messy first drafts** with all its imperfections, for its only job is to exist.

7. **Thou shalt not cloak thy words.** Abandon ye thy purple prose, excessive adjectives and adverbs, and passive sentences. Seek out precision and clarity. Let thy editor be thy guide.

8. **Thou shalt finish writing thy book** for the author who finishes shall raise his or her craft to a higher plain. He or she is free to write something new, something better.

9. **Thou shalt not self-publish thy book with shoddy covers and clumsy editing.** Woes (and poor book reviews) betide he or she who inflicts upon the world a pale imitation of a book, published only for gold.

10. **Thou shalt tell stories about thy book** to like-minded souls, for thy readers are waiting.

After you finish writing your non-fiction book and you can hold a published copy in your hands, email me a picture.

We shall spread the good words.

Write on,

– Bryan Collins

TOP TOOLS AND RESOURCES FOR TODAY'S AUTHORS

What follows in this section is a list of tools I use and rely on as an indie author.

The list is relatively long, and (depending on what your book is about) you won't need to use all of these tools.

If you're facing a technical problem, these tools can help.

Remember, writing your non-fiction book is more important than mastering any tool. So pick a useful tool and get back to writing and marketing your book.

If you're reading this on print or you want more information, you can find my always-up-to-date list blogging and writing tools at http://becomeawritertoday.com/writing-apps/.

FOR WRITING YOUR BOOK

Nuance Dragon Naturally Speaking

I use Dragon software to dictate early drafts of blog posts, book chapters and articles. This piece of software enables me to write faster, and it also reduces the amount of time I spend struggling with repetitive strain injury (RSI). In this article, I explain how to get started with dictation http://becomeawritertoday.com/speech-to-text

Evernote

If I have an idea for a book that I don't want to forget, I keep it in here. I also save articles I like into Evernote as part of my personal swipe file. Sometimes, I take photos of mind maps on my whiteboard with my phone and put them in Evernote too. It's my digital brain.

IA Writer

This is a useful minimalist writing app for Mac and iOS. The font Nitti Light is worth the price of admission alone. I use IA Writer for writing short articles on the go.

iMindMap

I've used these affordable tools to create mind maps in the past. They're easy to learn too. Alternatively, you can create a mind map using pen and paper. To see how I use mindmaps for writing, visit https://becomeawritertoday.com/mind-mapping/

A Moleskine notebook

No, there's no need to use a Moleskine notebook for writing or capturing ideas, but I'm drawn to the build quality of these notebooks and the feel of the paper. I've a box full of these near where I write.

Scrivener

I can't recommend Scrivener enough. I use it to write blog posts and books. I've used Scrivener to write feature articles for newspapers, reports, a thesis and books. Other useful writing apps include Ulysses, Pages and IA Writer. Get my free Scrivener blogging template at http://becomeawritertoday.com/using-scrivener-blogging-ultimate-guide/

Vellum

This application enables indie authors to edit and create professional looking books for every store and device with ease. I write books like this in Scrivener, export to Vellum, lay the book out and then create the relevant file for Amazon, Kobo, iTunes and so on. Sorry Windows fans, it's Mac-only for now.

FOR EDITING AND PROOFREADING

Autocrit

This is a critiquing tool for fiction writers. It costs $29 per month.

Grammarly

This is my proofreading and grammar checker application of choice. It costs $29.95 per month, but there are discounts available for quarterly and annual subscriptions. See https://becomeawritertoday.com/grammar-checker-review-grammarly/

After the Deadline

This is a somewhat less powerful but still useful alternative to Grammarly. It's free.

Kibin

Unlike many proofreading and editing services, Kibin will edit for grammar, spelling, punctuation, sentence structure and more. I've sent book chapters and articles to this service. See http://Kibin.com.

ProWritingAid

This software integrates with popular writing applications like Word and Scrivener. It costs $40 per year.

Hemingway Editor

If you're not a confident writer, don't worry. Hemingway App will review your text and, in the spirit of Ernest Hemingway, it will tell you what to remove or edit so your writing is bold and clear.

Reedsy

If you want to find a book editor, proof-reader or cover designer, Reedsy takes the hassle out of it. When you sign up, you get access to a community of self-publishing professionals that are ready to work with you and on your book. See http://Reedsy.com.

FOR COMMISSIONING A BOOK COVER

Reedsy enables authors to find editors, designs and more.

The Book Designer runs a monthly competition featuring some of the indie industry's best book cover designers. Find a cover you like and then contact them. Visit https://www.thebookdesigner.com/

I've used **99designs** to find a designer to create a book cover for one of my books. If you want a professional design (like a logo, business card or packaging) for your online business, 99designs is a good place to start too. See https://becomeawritertoday.com/99designs-competition/

The **Book Cover Designer** offers a large selection of pre-made covers that you can customise. Visit: thebookcoverdesigner.com.

Joanna Penn provides a list of book cover design resources on at thecreativepenn.com.

OTHER TOOLS I RECOMMEND FOR AUTHORS

A whiteboard

I keep a large whiteboard next to where I write. It's a great way of capturing and organising ideas. I also use it for mind maps and for creating outlines for articles, chapters and even books. I find a whiteboard less confining than traditional digital tools.

Audible

As a writer, your inputs (what you read, listen to and watch) are just as important as your outputs (what you write, paint or draw). I spend at least an hour a day listening to audiobooks that I purchased from Audible on my smartphone.

If you sign up, they'll give you your first audiobook for free. To learn more about creating your audiobook, please see https://becomeawritertoday.com/how-to-make-an-audiobook/

BookFunnel

If you want to send copies of your book to beta readers or distribute Advanced Reader Copies (ARC), use BookFunnel. Once you upload your files, send readers a link. It automatically provides them the correct version of your book alongside instructions about how to open it.

Brain.fm

Brain.fm provides AI-generated music for focus, relaxation and deep work. When I use this, I find I can enter a state of creative flow faster. Plug in a pair of headphones, and you're good to go.

Buffer

I use Buffer to share articles, photos and social media updates by myself and others on Instagram, Facebook, LinkedIn, Twitter and Pinterest. Buffer simplifies sharing social media updates across multiple networks and enables you to schedule your updates in advance. You can enable others to manage your social media profiles… leaving you more time to work on your creative projects.

Day One

For years, I wrote journal entries in a password-protected file in my computer. When I last checked, the file was over 150,000 words long, it took several seconds to open and was slow to navigate.

Now, I use Day One. It supports Markdown (a method for converting plain text to HTML) and pictures. It also simplifies finding older entries. There are versions for Mac and iOS.

Freedom

If you keep getting distracted while writing, use the app Freedom. It will disable your internet access for a pre-determined period, allowing you to focus on writing and not on cat videos!

G Suite

It's time to put the hard-drives and USB keys away. Essentially, G Suite enables me to send and receive emails from the becomeawritertoday.com domain (bryan[at]BecomeAWriterToday.com) using the Gmail interface.

I also get lots of additional cloud storage and can easily collaborate with other writers, editors and designers.

Google Forms/Survey Monkey

Both of these tools are great for capturing the opinions of beta and ARC readers. It only takes a few minutes to set up a survey, and you can send it to members of your email list (if you have one).

Kindle Spy

Kindle Spy is a great tool that will help you see what books are selling on Amazon and how much they earn. Then you can use this information to increase sales of your book.

KDP Rocket

KDPRocket is the other tool in my arsenal for doing market research and checking out what sells on Amazon.

LeadPages

I use LeadPages to create landing and squeeze pages for my books. I also use it to create sign-up forms for my mailing list. See https://becomeawritertoday.com/leadpages-review/

Logitech MX Master 2S/M510 Mouse

I use these wireless laser mice alongside gel-wrist supports. They help me avoid RSI.

Web-hosting

For your author website or blog, I suggest hosting with Siteground. If you need help, check out my detailed guide on how to start a blog: https://becomeawritertoday.com/start-a-blog/

Screenflow for Mac

This is a great tool for recording video and screencasts. It's also relatively simple to edit your recordings and export them to a format suitable for Facebook, YouTube or your website. Also consider Camtasia.

Sumo

Sumo is an all-in-one tool that enables you to gather email addresses, set up a share bar on the side of blog posts and also track how people interact with your work online.

If you're sharing your work online, I highly recommended it. See https://becomeawritertoday.com/sumome-review/

Upwork

No matter how talented or hard-working you are, it's impossible to do everything alone. Upwork is a great service for finding designers, editors and more who can help you with time-consuming tasks so you can spend more time writing books.

I've used Upwork to hire video-editors and also developers who fixed problems on my website.

PickFu
This poll service is useful for A/B testing book covers and titles.
VXi Headset
This affordable headset is purpose-built for dictation and when I switched to it, my accuracy dramatically increased.

REMEMBER YOUR BONUS

I've created a **FREE video masterclass**. It will help cut months off how long it takes you to write your book, using my best tactics and strategies.

WAIT!
DID YOU CLAIM YOUR FREE BONUS?

VISIT
BECOMEAWRITERTODAY.COM/AUTHOR

If you want to get this masterclass, visit http://becomeawritertoday.com/author

BECOME A WRITER TODAY

Yes, You Can Write!
101 Proven Writing Prompts that Will Help You Find Creative Ideas Faster for Your Journal, Blogging, Writing Your Book and More
(Book 1)

The Savvy Writer's Guide to Productivity
How to Work Less, Finish Writing Your Story or Book, and Find the Success You Deserve
(Book 2)

The Art of Writing a Non-Fiction Book
An Easy Guide to Researching, Creating, Editing, and Self-publishing Your First Book
(Book 3)

http://becomeawritertodaybook.com

THE POWER OF CREATIVITY

Learning How to Build Lasting Habits, Face Your Fears and Change Your Life
(Book 1)

An Uncommon Guide to Mastering Your Inner Genius and Finding New Ideas That Matter
(Book 2)

How to Conquer Procrastination, Finish Your Work and Find Success
(Book 3)

http://thepowerofcreativitybook.com

ABOUT THE AUTHOR

In this life, Bryan Collins is an author.

In another life, he worked as a journalist and a radio producer. Before that, he plucked chickens. He is passionate about helping people accomplish more with their writing projects, and when he's not writing, he's running.

At becomeawritertoday.com, Bryan offers new writers practical advice about writing, creativity, productivity and more. His work has appeared on Fast Company, Lifehacker and Copyblogger.

Bryan holds a degree in communications and journalism, a diploma in social care, a master's degree in disability studies and a diploma in digital media.

You can reach him on Twitter @BryanJCollins, via email at bryan@becomeawritertoday.com or join his Become a Writer Today Facebook page.

Bryan is also the author of the novella *Poor Brother, Rich Brother* and a three-part series: *The Power of Creativity*.

He lives an hour outside of Dublin.

becomeawritertoday.com
bryan@becomeawritertoday.com

For A

ACKNOWLEDGMENTS

I'd like to thank the following early readers: Arulnathan John, Kieran Lynch, Nicholas Reicher, Susan Johnson from thrivingamidstchoas.com, and Martine Ellis.

I'd also like to acknowledge Crystal W. from Kibin Editing, Sean Sabo as a proofreader, Saskia Nicol for the book cover, and Marko Babic for preparing the audiobook.

© 2017, 2018 by Bryan Collins.

Reproduction in whole or part of this publication without express consent is strictly prohibited.

The Art of Writing a Non-Fiction Book
An Easy Guide to Researching, Creating, Editing, and Self-publishing Your First Book

Become a Writer Today

REFERENCES

BOOKS

Allen, David. *Getting Things Done*. 2011.

Bukowski, Charles. *The Pleasures of the Damned Selected Poems 1951-1993*. HaperCollins. 2007.

Cheever, John. *The Journals*. 2011.

Chesterton, G.K. *Charles Dickens: A Critical Study*. Kessenger Publishing. 2005.

Currey, Mason. *Daily Rituals: How Great Minds Make Time, Fine Inspiration and Get to Work*. Picador. 2013.

Coyne, Shawn. *The Story Grid*. Black Irish Books. 2015.

Ferris, Tim. *The 4-Hour Work Week: Escape the 9-5, Live Anywhere and Join the New Rich*. Harmony. 2007.

REFERENCES

Feynman, Richard P. *Surely You're Joking, Mr. Fenyman!* Vintage. 1992.

Godin, Seth. *Tribes: We Need You to Lead Us.* Hachette Digital. 2008.

Gladwell, Michael. *The Tipping Point: How Little Things Can Make a Big Difference.* Back Bay Books. 2002.

Goldberg, Natalie. *Writing Down the Bones: Freeing the Writer Within.* Shambhala. 2010.

Halbert, Gary C. *The Boron Letters.* Bond Halbert Publishing. 2013.

King, Stephen. *On Writing: A Memoir of the Craft.* Scribner. 2010.

McDougall, Christopher. *Born to Run: Hidden Tribe, Superathletes, and the Greatest Race the World Has Never Seen.* Vintage. 2011.

McKee, Robert. *Story: Substance, Structure, Style and the Principles of Screenwriting.* HarperCollins. 1997.

Nabokov, Vladimir. *Speak, Memory: An Autobiography Revised.* Penguin Classics. 2012.

Pressfield, Stephen. *The War of Art: Break Through the Blocks and Win Your Inner Creative Battles.* Black Irish Entertainment. 2012.

Schwarzenegger, Arnold. *Total Recall: My Unbelievably True Life Story.* Fitness Publications. 2012.

Stein, Sol. *Stein On Writing: A Master Editor of Some of the Most Successful Writers of Our Century Shares His Craft Techniques and Strategies.* McMillan USA. 2014.

Woolf, Virginia. *A Writer's Diary (1918-1941).* e-arrtnow. 2014.

REFERENCES

Zoe Segal, Gillian. *Getting There*. Harry N. Abrams, 2015.

ARTICLES

Als, Hilton. *"Joan Didion, The Art of Nonfiction No. 1."* Paris Review. Spring 2006. Accessed at https://www.theparisreview.org/interviews/5601/joan-didion-theart-of-nonfiction-no-1-joan-didion.

American Psychological Association. "Multitasking: Switching Costs." *American Psychological Association*. 2006. Accessed at *http://www.apa.org/research/action/multitask.aspx on January 29, 2017.*

Author Earnings. *"May 2016 Author Earnings Report: The Definitive Million-Title Study of US Author Earnings."* Author Earnings. 2017. Accessed at http://authorearnings.com/report/may-2016-report/ on January 28, 2017.

Cunningham, Anne E., and Keith E. Stanovich. *"What Reading Does for the Mind."* Journal of Direct Instruction. University of California, Berkley. 1998. Accessed at http://mccleskeyms.typepad.com/files/what-reading-does-for-the-mind.pdf on March 27, 2017.

Desta, Yohana. *"10 Famous Writers Who Don't Use Modern Tech to Create."* Mashable.com. February 15, 2014. Accessed at http://mashable.com/2014/02/15/modernwriters-technology/#DijnxwtYZkqd on January 28, 2017.

Gladwell, Michael. *"Hi, I'm Malcolm Gladwell, author of The Tipping Point, Blink, Outliers and--most recently--David and Goliath: Underdogs, Misfits and the Art of Battling Giants. Ask me anything!"* Reddit. June 2, 2014. Accessed at

REFERENCES

https://www.reddit.com/r/IAmA/comments/2740ct/hi_im_malcolm_gladwell_author_of_the_tipping/ on September 26, 2017.

Greene, Robert. *"I am Robert Greene, author of The 48 Laws of Power, The Art of Seduction, and others -- AMA."* Reddit. April 18, 2013. Accessed at https://www.reddit.com/r/IAmA/comments/1cmb0d/i_am_robert_greene_author_of_the_48_laws_of_power/ on January 28, 2017.

Office for National Statistics, United Kingdom. *"United Kingdom; Office for National Statistics (UK); 2011 to 2014; 42,000*; UK households . Total Number of authors, Writers and Translators in the United Kingdom (UK) from 2011 to 2014 (in 1,000)."* Statista. 2017.

McGrath, Matt. *"Wood Density Key to Violin Sound."* BBC. July 2, 2008. Accessed at http://news.bbc.co.uk/2/hi/science/nature/7484975.stm on January 28, 2017.

Mueller, Pam and Daniel M. Oppenheimer. *"The Pen Is Mightier Than the Keyboard: Advantages of Longhand over Laptop Note Taking."* Psychological Science 25, no. 6 (April 23, 2014): 1159-68. Accessed at https://sites.udel.edu/victorp/files/2010/11/Psychological-Science-2014-Mueller-0956797614524581-1u0h0yu.pdf on February 14, 2017.

Nelson, Kelyse. *"How Much Does It Cost to Self-Publish a Book?"* Bookpromotion.com. 2015. Accessed at www.bookpromotion.com/how-much-does-it-cost-to-self-publish-a-book/ on April 26, 2017.

Sitar, Dana. The Write Life. 2015. *"How Much Does It Cost to Self-Publish a Book? 4 Authors Share Their Numbers"*. Accessed at thewritelife.com/cost-to-self-publish-a-book/#.j0dxzg:Xy7M on April 26, 2017.

Vonnegut, Kurt. *"8 Rules for Writing."* New York Writers' Intensive. Accessed on http://newyorkwritersintensive.com/morningpages/kurt-vonneguts-8-rules-for-writing/ on January 28, 2017.

US Bureau of Labor Statistics United States. *"Bureau of Labor Statistics; 2011 to 2015; Excluding Self-Employed Workers."* Statista. 2017.

Weinberg, Dana Beth. *"Lessons and Expectations as the Digital Book World and Writer's Digest Author Survey Evolves."* DBW. 2014. Accessed at http://www.digitalbookworld.com/2014/lessons-and-expectationsas-the-digital-book-world-and-writers-digest-author-surveyevolves/ on January 28, 2017.

Weinschenk, Susan. *"The True Cost of Multi-Tasking."* Psychology Today. September 18, 2012. Accessed at https://www.psychologytoday.com/blog/brain-wise/201209/the-true-cost-multi-tasking on August 5, 2017.

Printed in Great Britain
by Amazon